THAT YOU MIGHT HAVE LIFE

An Introduction to the Paschal Mystery of Christ

FORMED IN CHRIST SERIES

About the Series

Who is Jesus Christ? What does it mean to know him? What do the Church and her sacraments have to do with him? How are we to follow him?

These are the questions at the heart of the Catholic faith, and these are the questions the Formed in Christ series answers. Rooted in the story of Salvation History and steeped in the writings of the Fathers and Doctors of the Church, this series of high school textbooks from the St. Paul Center seeks to engage minds and hearts as it presents the tenets of the Catholic faith in Scripture and Tradition.

Over the course of this comprehensive, four-year curriculum, students will learn the fundamentals of Church teaching on the Person and mission of Jesus Christ, Sacred Scripture, the Church, the sacraments, morality, Church history, vocations, Catholic social teaching, and more. Just as important, they'll be invited, again and again, to enter more deeply into a relationship with Christ, growing in love of him as they grow in knowledge of him.

Published

Evidence of Things Unseen: An Introduction to Fundamental Theology
Andrew Willard Jones and Louis St. Hilaire.
Edited by Stimpson Chapman

The Word Became Flesh: An Introduction to Christology
Andrew Willard Jones. Edited by Emily Stimpson Chapman

That You Might Have Life: An Introduction to the Paschal Mystery of Christ
Louis St. Hilaire. Edited by Emily Stimpson Chapman

I Will Build My Church: An Introduction to Ecclesiology
Andrew Willard Jones. Edited by Emily Stimpson Chapman

Do This in Remembrance: An Introduction to the Sacraments
Jacob Wood. Edited by Emily Stimpson Chapman

Christ Alive in Us: An Introduction to Moral Theology
John Meinert and Emily Stimpson Chapman

THAT YOU MIGHT HAVE LIFE

An Introduction to the Paschal Mystery of Christ

LOUIS ST. HILAIRE

Edited by Emily Stimpson Chapman

EMMAUS ROAD PUBLISHING

www.emmausroad.org

Steubenville, Ohio

In Grateful Recognition of Lawrence Joseph & Lynn Marie Blanford

Emmaus Road Publishing
1468 Parkview Circle
Steubenville, Ohio 43952

Printed in the United States of America

Library of Congress Control Number: 2019934890

ISBN 978-1-949013-41-2

Cover image: *The Ascension*, Giovanni Bernardino Azzolino (1572–1645)

Cover design and layout by Margaret Ryland

TABLE OF CONTENTS

Part I

The Goodness of Creation and Our Fall from Grace

From all eternity, God has had a plan for your happiness. That's what he wants for you: happiness, beatitude, and eternal joy. Every moment of your life, he is working in some way to lead you closer to that joy, which ultimately means closer to him, the source of all joy. He is doing the same for every person you know and don't know. He wants every member of the human race to know eternal happiness. Despite our sin, despite our woundedness and brokenness and all the ways we fall short of who God made us to be, he still loves us and he still wants us in heaven with him.

God accomplishes this plan through his only begotten Son, Jesus Christ. Two thousand years ago God became man so that we could live forever. He took on human flesh and a human nature so that we could know who he is, how much he loves us, and what he wants for us. In Jesus, we see the fullness of divine Revelation.

In this course, we're going to look more closely at the mission of Jesus Christ. We'll look at why God became man, how he prepared humanity to receive the gift of the Incarnation, how he set about fulfilling his mission during his life on earth, and how he brought about the culmination of that mission on the Cross. We'll also look at how each of us participates in his mission, as disciples and in the life of the Church.

First, however, we need to go back to the beginning of human history in order to understand why the mission of Jesus Christ was necessary.

Chapter 1

The Creation of the World and Our First Parents

Assigned Reading
Genesis 1

How to Read the Creation Story

The story of Jesus' mission begins in the Book of Genesis, when God created the heavens, the earth, and the first human beings—Adam and Eve. To correctly understand the truth God intends to teach us in Genesis, we have to learn to read the book correctly. This requires overcoming certain common misunderstandings about the creation story.

As you learned in previous courses, God inspired human authors to use their gifts to compose the Sacred Scriptures. You also learned that if we want to understand those inspired texts correctly, we need to look at the Scriptures' historical context and the literary forms the sacred writers used. When we do this, we can see that it's a mistake to read the creation story as if it were a modern science or history textbook. Genesis' primary purpose isn't to convey scientific facts, but rather to teach the religious truth about creation—its origin in God, its order, and its goodness—and the religious truth about man—our vocation, the origin of sin, and our hope for salvation(CCC 289). In other words,

Genesis seeks to give us the "why" behind the world—why we exist, why we suffer, why we always long for more. These aren't scientific problems; they're spiritual problems, and we have to read Genesis with this understanding (CCC 284).

This is important, because while science can describe the physical processes by which the world and living beings came to be, it can't answer deeper questions about our origin and purpose. It's these truths that Genesis reveals. It tells the true story of how the world, humanity, and sin came to exist. Importantly, though, it doesn't tell that story like a documentary would. Rather, it tells the story as a painting or a poem might. While Genesis does tell us about things that really happened (God *did* create the heavens and the earth; the first humans *were* in friendship with God and lost that friendship through sin), it does so using poetic, figurative, and symbolic language to convey these theological truths (CCC 362, 375, 390, 396).

God Created Everything That Is

The first several verses of the creation story are perhaps some of the most familiar words in the Bible, but we don't want to just pass over them, for they reveal some of the deepest and most important truths about creation and God himself.

> In the beginning God created the heavens and the earth. The earth was without form and void, and darkness was upon the face of the deep; and the Spirit of God was moving over the face of the waters.
>
> And God said, "Let there be light"; and there was light. And God saw that the light was good; and God separated the light from the darkness. God called the light Day, and the darkness he called Night. And there was evening and there was morning, one day. (Gen 1:1–5)

The first thing these lines tell us is that God created "the heavens and the earth." In other words, God created everything we see, from the sky and stars above ("the heavens") to the earth below our feet. Moreover, if we think of "heaven" as indicating spiritual realities and "earth" as indicating the material world, we also can understand this as meaning that God created all of reality—both spiritual and material (CCC 326). Ultimately, what this means is that God created absolutely everything there is. Nothing exists that does not come from him.

Also, unlike ancient polytheistic myths, which claimed that multiple gods or spiritual realities existed and were part of the created world or embodied in different parts of it, Genesis teaches that the entire universe—visible and invisible—comes from the one God. He alone is uncreated—no one created him, nor did he create himself. He is not himself a part of the created world. He is not another "thing" inside the universe, but rather is the source of everything.

God Gives Everything Form and Order

The first passages of Genesis also tell us that the earth begins "without form" and "void." Right away, however, God begins to set things in order, distinguishing light from darkness (Gen 1:4), the sky from the seas, and the heavens from the earth (Gen 1:6–10).

From this, we can see that the world we experience is magnificently ordered. This order is so deep and pervasive that we usually take it for granted. Without even thinking about it, we expect the sun to rise in the east every morning, and we expect the laws of physics to work consistently in every time and place in the universe so that we can accurately throw a football or predict the movements of stars millions of miles away.

Even when the natural world appears chaotic, we expect that we can discover deeper patterns with careful observation and thought. The entire work of science—discovering patterns in nature and formulating scientific laws that describe them—is based on this order. In a profound way, the universe is open to being discovered and comprehended by the human mind. Why, though?

Genesis answers that question by revealing that this order comes from the divine mind of God. It makes sense then that it can be discovered by the created minds of human beings, which are a reflection of their Creator.

It's also important to note that in Genesis, God creates and sets things in order simply by speaking. This shows that God is all-powerful, so at his mere word, all creation comes into being. It's also important because later, in the New Testament, we learn that God's Word, through whom all things were made, is his Son, the Second Person of the Trinity:

> In the beginning was the Word, and the Word was with God, and the Word was God. He was in the beginning with God; all things were made through him, and without him was not anything made that was made. (John 1:1–3)

In the Greek version of the New Testament, the word for "Word" is *logos*, which is the source of the English word "logic." Thus, the order or "logic" of the universe derives from the Logos himself, the Son of God, through whom the universe was created.

This also helps us see that the creation event is the work of all three Persons of the Holy Trinity (CCC 290–292). God the Father is the First Person of the Holy Trinity and the source of all that is—like a human father is the source of life of his children. God the Son, the Second Person of the Trinity, is the Word through which creation is spoken into being, giving everything order. Finally, according to Genesis 1:2, the Spirit of God—the Holy Spirit, who is the Third Person of the Trinity—"was moving over the face of the waters."

God Created All that Is, Seen and Unseen

God is perfect. Unlike finite beings like us who depend upon God and other creatures to survive and feel fulfilled, God doesn't need anything or anyone. He is complete in himself. Thus, he didn't need to create the world. He freely chose to do so in order to both share his love and goodness and to show his glory.

> Scripture and Tradition never cease to teach and celebrate this fundamental truth: "The world was made for the glory of God" [*Dei Filius*, can. § 5: DS 3025]. St. Bonaventure explains that God created all things "not to increase his glory, but to show it forth and to communicate it" [St. Bonaventure, *In II Sent.* I, 2, 2, 1], for God has no other reason for creating than his love and goodness: "Creatures came into existence when the key of love opened his hand" [St. Thomas Aquinas, *Sent.* II, Prol.]. (CCC 293)

We see the glory, love, and goodness of God reflected in everything he has created. As we read in Genesis, God created the heavens and the earth (Gen 1:1), and we can understand this as meaning that he created both the spiritual and material world. Similarly, in the Creed, we confess that God is the Creator of all things, "visible and invisible."

The "visible" world refers not just to things that we can see with our eyes, but also to everything that we can detect with our senses—in other words, the entire material universe, including everything that can be known through the natural sciences, such as energy, physical forces and fields, time and space, and the laws by which they interact. All these things are part of the visible universe created by God.

"Invisible" refers to spiritual realities. Now, God himself is invisible. He doesn't have the physical properties of material things, and we can't detect him by our senses or in any observable way through scientific experiments. God is also uncreated. Nobody created him, including himself. God did, however, create the angels.

The word "angel" comes from the Greek word *angelos,* which means "messenger." The angels are purely spiritual, nonmaterial beings who serve as the servants and messengers of God. This is often the role we see them playing in Scripture.

> Angels have been present since creation and throughout the history of salvation, announcing this salvation from afar or near and serving the accomplishment of the divine plan: they closed the earthly paradise; protected Lot; saved Hagar and her child; stayed Abraham's hand; communicated the law by their minis-

> try; led the People of God; announced births and callings; and assisted the prophets, just to cite a few examples [Cf. *Job* 38:7 (where angels are called "sons of God"); *Gen* 3:24; 19; 21:17; 22:11; *Acts* 7:53; *Ex* 23:20–23; *Judg* 13; 6:11–24; *Isa* 6:6; *1 Kings* 19:5]. Finally, the angel Gabriel announced the birth of the Precursor and that of Jesus himself [Cf. *Lk* 1:11, 26]. (CCC 332)

The angels surrounded, served, and adored Jesus throughout his life, glorifying God at his birth (Luke 2:13–14), ministering to him in the desert (Matt 4:11), strengthening him in the Garden of Gethsemane (Luke 22:43), and proclaiming his Resurrection to those who visited his tomb (Mark 16:5–7). Someday angels will announce Jesus' return and serve him at his judgment (Matt 24:31; CCC 333). In the meantime, the angels continue to intercede for and defend the Church and individual believers (Matt 18:10; CCC 336).

SELECTED READING

Pope Benedict XVI, *Papal Audience on Creation*, Paul VI Audience Hall, February 6, 2013

The Creed which begins by describing God as "the Father Almighty," the topic of our meditation last week, then adds that he is "Maker of heaven and earth," and thus takes up the affirmation with which the Bible begins. Indeed the first verse of Sacred Scripture reads: "In the beginning God created the heavens and the earth" (Gen 1:1). God is the origin of all things and his omnipotence as a loving Father unfolds in the beauty of the creation.

In creation, God manifested himself as Father, since he is the origin of life, and in creating he shows his omnipotence. And Sacred Scripture uses very evocative images of it (cf. Is 40:12; 45:18; 48:13; Ps 104:2.5; 135:7; Prov 8:27–9; Job 38–39). As a good and powerful Father, he takes care of what he has created with unfailing love and faithfulness, as the Psalms say over and over again (cf. Ps 57:11; 108:5; 36:6). So it is that creation becomes a place in which to know and recognize the Lord's omnipotence and goodness, as well as an appeal to our faith as believers that we proclaim God as Creator.

"By faith," the author of the Letter to the Hebrews wrote, "we understand that the world was created by the word of God, so that what is seen was made out of things which do not appear" (11:3). Faith thus implies the ability to recognize the invisible, by identifying its traces in the visible world. Believers can read the great book of nature and understand its language (cf. Ps 19:2–5); but the word of revelation that awakens faith is necessary if man is to become fully aware of the reality of God as Creator and Father. The Book of Sacred Scripture says that human intelligence can find the clue to understanding the world in the light of faith.

With the solemn presentation of the divine work of creation that unfolded over seven days, the first chapter of Genesis in particular occupies a special place. God brought the creation to completion in six days and on the seventh, the sabbath, he did not do anything, but rested: a day of freedom for all, a day of communion with God. Thus, with this image the Book of Genesis tells us that God's first thought was to find a love that would correspond to his love.

Then his second thought was to create a material world in which to place this love, these creatures who respond to him in freedom. This structure therefore results in the text being marked by certain meaningful repetitions. For example, the sentence "God saw that it was good," is repeated six times (vv. 4, 10, 12, 18, 21, 25) and to conclude, the seventh time, after the creation of man: "God saw everything that he had made, and behold, it was very good" (v. 31). Everything that God creates is beautiful and good, steeped in wisdom and love; God's creative action brings order, instills harmony, and bestows beauty.

In the narrative of Genesis, therefore, it becomes clear that the Lord created with his word: ten times we read in the text the phrase: "God said" (vv. 3, 6, 9, 11, 14, 20, 24, 26, 28, 29). It is the Word, the *Logos* of God who is at the origin of the reality of the world, and saying: "God said," it was so, emphasizes the effective power of the divine Word. This is what the Psalmist sings: "by the word of the Lord the heavens were made, and all their host by the breath of his mouth . . . for he spoke, and it came to be, he commanded and it stood forth" (33[32]:6, 9). Life springs forth, the world exists, because all things obey the divine Word.

However our question today is: in the age of science and technology does speaking of creation still make sense? How should we understand the narratives in Genesis? The Bible does not intend to be a natural science manual; rather, it wishes to make the authentic and profound truth of things understood. The fundamental truth that the accounts of Genesis reveal to us is that the world is not a collection of forces that clash with each other; it has its origin and its permanence in the *Logos,* in God's eternal Reason which continues to sustain the universe.

A plan of the world exists which is conceived by this Reason, by the Creator Spirit. To believe that this is the foundation of all things illuminates every aspect of existence and gives us the courage to face the adventure of life with trust and hope. Therefore, Scripture tells us that the origin of being, of the world, our own origin is not in the irrational or in need, but rather in reason and love and freedom. Consequently, there is this alternative: either the priority of the irrational, of necessity, or the priority of reason, of freedom, of love. We believe in the latter hypothesis.

QUESTIONS FOR REVIEW

1. What questions does the creation account in Genesis seek to answer? What questions does it not seek to answer?
2. What do we mean when we say God is the creator of all things "visible and invisible"?
3. Through whom did God create the world?
4. Who created God?
5. What are angels?

QUESTIONS FOR DISCUSSION

1. What are some examples of questions science can't answer? What does this teach us about the limits of science?
2. When you look around at the created world, what evidence do you see for God's existence?
3. What does it mean that God has given order to creation? What are some of the consequences of this?

Chapter 2

Human Beings: the Summit of Creation

Assigned Reading
Genesis 2

In the Image and Likeness of God

The story of creation in Genesis culminates in the creation of human beings. All creation reflects God's glory, but the human person does so uniquely, for we, and we alone, were created in God's image and likeness. Unlike everything else in the visible world, only human beings are persons, reflecting God's immortality, rationality, and freedom. Alone among the creatures on earth, only human beings have a spiritual and immortal soul and can know and love God and share in his life (CCC 356–357, 1701, 1704–1705).

Because human beings are created in the image of God and are called to share in God's own life, we have a unique dignity that surpasses that of all other things on earth. Simply because we exist, each of us is worthy of love and respect (CCC 1702–1703, 1706). This means we have a dignity that comes not from what we say or do, not from what we look like or how we dress, not from how smart we are, how talented we are, or how rich we are, but from the simple fact that God made us in his image and wants us to spend our eternity with him.

As God's living image, we also are his stewards on earth. God created the earth for us. It is his gift to us and was designed to meet all our needs—for food, shelter, warmth, and more. He also gave us dominion over the world, entrusting us with the rule of creation (Gen 1:26, 28). This dominion doesn't mean we can exploit creation carelessly or for selfish purposes. Rather, God wants us to act as good stewards—or caretakers—of this gift so that others (today and in future generations) can enjoy its fruits and so that we can offer all of it back to God in thanksgiving (CCC 358, 373).

This, the Bible tells us, is how it was in the beginning, after God created the first man and the first woman.

Male and Female He Created Them

Genesis 2:4–25 retells the story of creation in order to explain in more detail God's creation of human beings and his plan for us. Remember, just as with Genesis 1, this is a poetic explanation of the origin of man and woman, rich with figurative language, so we shouldn't read it as if were a science or history textbook or read the details as contradicting Genesis 1.

First, when we look at Genesis 2:18–25, we see in more detail how God created us as male and female. The Catechism explains the significance of this:

> Man and woman have been *created*, which is to say, *willed* by God: on the one hand, in perfect equality as human persons; on the other, in their respective beings as man and woman. "Being man" or "being woman" is a reality which is good and willed by God: man and woman possess an inalienable dignity which comes to them immediately from God their Creator [Cf. *Gen* 2:7, 22]. Man and woman are both with one and the same dignity "in the image of God." In their "being-man" and "being-woman," they reflect the Creator's wisdom and goodness. (CCC 369)

The first lesson that comes when we read Genesis 2:18–25 together with Genesis 1:27 is that man and woman were created together in the image of God. While God himself, as a purely spiritual being, is neither male nor female, man and woman in our differences both reflect something of God's infinite perfection (CCC 370, 2335). As such, both sexes are equally created in the image of God and are therefore equal in dignity (CCC 2334).

The second lesson from these passages is that man and woman were created for each other. We are equal, but we are not the same. Differences between us—in our bodies and our souls—exist. But these differences are good. They allow us to complement each other and draw us together (CCC 371), making it possible for us to more fully reflect the image of God. As God says in Genesis 2:18, "It is not good that man should be alone." God himself, remember, is a communion of three divine Persons, a Holy Trinity in which each member gives themselves completely to the other in an eternal exchange of life-giving love. Because of this, the image of God in humanity shines forth in an especially powerful way in the communion of human persons (CCC 372, 1702), and most powerfully of all in the marriage of man and woman. In marriage, man and woman are united so closely that they become "one flesh" (Gen 2:24). They make a complete gift of themselves to each other, and when they do, their love becomes life-giving. It literally gives life to a third person, a child (CCC 2335). In this way, mother, father, and children reflect the Trinity—a communion of persons, united in a love that is generous and life-giving.

This reveals the true purpose of human sexuality. The physical desire we feel for each other and the pleasure we experience in sex is meant to draw man and woman together into this fruitful communion of lifelong, life-giving love. It's meant to move us to love, to marry, and to bring new life into the world. Sex isn't just about our own personal pleasure. It's not simply about satisfying our own desires. When we treat sex that way, it actually divides man and woman because we end up using the other person as a means to our own pleasure. Only in marriage, where there is total commitment, the total gift of self, and the desire to cooperate with God in bringing forth new life, can human sexuality flourish as God made it to flourish. Only in marriage can sex bring us the joy and fulfillment that it's meant to bring us, uniting man and woman in an act of true communion.

Achieving this communion requires the virtue of chastity, which frees us from being dominated by sexual passions. Chastity allows a husband and wife to direct their sexual love toward complete, lifelong self-giving and responsible parenthood, and frees the unmarried to give themselves in service and witness to their neighbors. It blossoms in the communion of friendship (CCC 2346–2347).

In this way, our nature as male and female points all of us, in every state of life, toward the love, self-giving, and communion with others that reflects the Holy Trinity. Men and women, in our similarities and differences, both bring gifts to the world and to the Church. Reflecting God's image each in our own way, we build up the Church in fulfilling our vocations.

Body and Soul

Genesis 2:7 reveals another way in which human beings are unique among God's creations. As we've learned, God created the heavens and the earth, the visible world of purely material beings and the invisible world of purely spiritual beings. In Genesis 2:7, we see that God forms man out of the dust of the earth; so, man is a material being, like everything else in the physical world. But God doesn't stop there. Unlike everything else he created, God brings man to life by breathing his own breath into man's nostrils.

The idea of breath is closely related to the ideas of "soul" and "spirit." In Hebrew, the word translated as "living being" (*nephesh*) can also mean "breath," and in other contexts is translated as "soul." Similarly, the English word "spirit" derives from a word that originally meant "breath." Consequently, we can see this scene as revealing how God, through his "Breath" (the Holy Spirit) creates man with both a body and a soul. Alone among creation, man is both a material and spiritual being—uniting in himself the visible and the invisible world (CCC 362).

The word "soul" is used in Scripture in a few different ways. In both Hebrew (*nephesh*) and Greek (*psyche*), the words often translated as "soul" can also be used to mean "life" or to refer to the entire human person. Most often though, we use it to mean our innermost self, the spiritual aspect of our being, which more than any other part of us reflects the image of God (CCC 363).

It's important to note that in Genesis 2:7 man's soul comes immediately from God. It doesn't arise out of the matter from which his body was formed. In fact, because it's spiritual, the human soul can't come from material things. Because of this, the Church teaches that every human soul is immediately created by God. Likewise, the spiritual soul does not break down after death like the human body, but is immortal (CCC 366).

Even so, the soul alone is only one part of the human person. A complete human being is both body and soul. Body and soul form a profound unity. The body, Pope St. John Paul II wrote in his theology of the body, "expresses the person" and "reveals the living soul."[1] It makes visible the invisible truths about who we are, and as such, it isn't just a shell we inhabit but is really and truly us. We are our bodies. Our bodies are us. Therefore, how we treat our bodies matters. What we do in and with our bodies has profound consequences for our souls. Both share in the dignity that comes from being made in "the image of God" and both experience redemption through Jesus. Indeed, Scripture tells us, the body of the baptized is a temple of the Holy Spirit (1 Cor 6:19–20), and at the final resurrection, the soul will be reunited with the body so that the whole person will share in the life of heaven (CCC 364–365).

Original Holiness and Justice

After God formed the first man from the dust of the earth and breathed life into him, he placed him in the garden. There, man and woman enjoyed friendship with God. God spoke with them directly and walked with them (Gen 3:8). Because Adam and Eve were without sin, God didn't

[1] Pope John Paul II, *Man and Woman He Created Them: A Theology of the Body*, trans. Michael Waldstein (Boston: Pauline Books and Media, 2006), 14:4.

give them extensive laws to obey. Instead, he asked them to follow just one simple command: "You may freely eat of every tree of the garden; but of the tree of the knowledge of good and evil you shall not eat, for in the day that you eat of it you shall die" (Gen 2:16–17). As long as they obeyed that command and remained in friendship with God, he promised, they would be free from suffering and death (CCC 376).

In this time in the Garden, before sin entered it, there was harmony. Man and woman experienced harmony with each other, forming "one flesh" (Gen 2:24). They also experienced harmony with the rest of creation, freely eating of the trees of the garden, tilling and keeping it, and giving names to the living creatures (Gen 2:15–16, 19). Perhaps most significantly, they experienced harmony within themselves. They were free both from sin and from the tendency toward sin, so they had mastery over themselves. They were truly free, in the sense that they could freely follow God's command and do what was right without the inner temptation and torment of sin. For Adam and Eve, in the beginning, doing the right thing was easy and natural. This state of harmony is called "original justice" (CCC 376–377).

This state (portrayed in figurative language in Gen 2) was God's original plan for human beings, and all of creation reflected it. Marriage, work, prayer—all was a gift and not a burden (CCC 378).

SELECTED READING

Pope Benedict XVI, *Papal Audience on Creation*, Paul VI Audience Hall, February 6, 2013

However, I would also like to say a word about the summit of all creation: man and woman, the human being, the only being "able to know and love his creator" (Pastoral Constitution on the Church in the Modern World, *Gaudium et Spes*, n. 12). Looking up at the heavens the Psalmist wondered: "when I look at your heavens, the work of your fingers, the moon and the stars which you have established; what is man that you are mindful of him, and the son of man that you care for him?" (Ps 8:3–4).

The human being, lovingly created by God, is indeed tiny in comparison with the immensity of the universe. At times, as we look with fascination at the enormous expanses of the firmament, we too perceive our limitations. Human beings are inhabited by this paradox: our smallness and our transience exist side by side with the greatness of what God's eternal love wanted for us.

The accounts of the Creation in the Book of Genesis also usher us in to this mysterious environment, helping us to become acquainted with God's plan for man. They affirm, first of all, that God formed man of dust from the ground (cf. Gen 2:7). This means that we are not God, we did not make ourselves, we are earth; yet it also means that we come from the good earth through the work of the good Creator.

In addition there is another fundamental reality: *all* human beings are dust, over and above the distinctions made by culture and by history, over and above every social difference; we are one humanity modeled with God's one earth.

Then there is a second element: the human being came into existence because God breathed the breath of life into the body he had formed from earth (cf. Gen 2:7). The human being is made in God's image and likeness (cf. Gen 1:26–27). For this reason we all bear within us the life-giving breath of God and every human life—the Bible tells us—is under God's special protection. This is the most profound reason for the inviolability of human dignity against every attempt to evaluate the person according to utilitarian and power-based criteria. To be in the image and likeness of God indicates that man is not closed in himself but has in God an essential reference point.

QUESTIONS FOR REVIEW

1. What does it mean for man to be a steward of creation?
2. What sets the human person apart from all the other creatures of the earth?
3. How do married persons and families image God?

4. A human person is a perfect union of what two things?
5. What do we call the original state of harmony that existed in the Garden?

QUESTIONS FOR DISCUSSION

1. What are some ways we can be good stewards of creation?
2. If every person is the image of God, what does that tell us about how we should treat one another?
3. How have you seen the differences between men and women divide us? How have you seen the differences between us unite us and help us?

Chapter 3

The Fall from Grace: Original Sin

Assigned Reading
Genesis 3:1–24

The original holiness and harmony of our first parents in the Garden of Eden that we read about in Genesis 2 is quite different from the life we know today. Genesis 3 explains how human beings lost this original state through sin.

Like the story of creation told in the first two chapters of Genesis, the story of the fall in Genesis 3 uses poetic and symbolic language. This doesn't mean that the story of the fall is just a myth, with no relationship to history or reality. The fundamental things about which it teaches us really did happen: our first parents *were* created in friendship with God, they *did* lose that friendship through sin, and profound consequences for the entire human race, which descends from them, *did* follow. However, just as with the first two chapters of Genesis, we don't read Genesis 3 like a news report or a history textbook. Instead, we have to examine the figurative language in Genesis 3 to see how it reveals the theological significance of these events (see "How to Read the Creation Story," in Chapter 1).

The Tempter and Temptation

The trouble in the garden began with the serpent, who tempted Eve to disobey God. This tempter was Satan (also called "the devil"). Satan is a fallen angel. He was created good by God, but at some point, he and the other fallen angels (or "demons") sinned, radically and permanently rejecting God and his reign. In the story of the tempting of Eve, we see how Satan and the other fallen angels have sought to lead human beings away from God from the very beginning. Satan even tried to tempt Jesus away from his mission (CCC 391–394).

It is important to know, however, that Satan and the other fallen angels are limited in their power. They have power as spiritual beings, but they are still just creatures. Only God is all-powerful. God allowed Satan to tempt our first parents, and God continues to allow him to tempt us, but God has the power to protect us from Satan if we turn to him. Moreover, while the struggle against Satan continues in this life, we know that Jesus has won the final victory (CCC 395).

Going back to the garden, we saw in Genesis 2 how Adam and Eve lived: they were free from sin, suffering, and death. Nevertheless, limits remained upon what they could do:

> The LORD God commanded the man, saying, "You may freely eat of every tree of the garden; but of the tree of the knowledge of good and evil you shall not eat, for in the day that you eat of it you shall die." (Gen 2:16–17)

Adam and Eve were made in the image of God, but they were still creatures made by God, with limits and boundaries placed on them by an all-knowing and loving creator. The Catechism tells us that the tree of the knowledge of good and evil "symbolically evokes the insurmountable limits that man, being a creature, must freely recognize and respect with trust" (CCC 396).

Of course, one might wonder why God put the tree in the garden in the first place, giving Adam and Eve the possibility of turning from him and bringing death upon themselves. Here, Genesis conveys an important aspect of God's relationship with our first parents and with us: God guides us and gives us commands, he desires us to love him, but he also gives us free will. God made man truly free—free even to reject him. This is important, because if we didn't have the ability to say no to God, then we would be mere puppets or robots. We would be incapable of really loving God, because love is always a gift, freely given.

God is good. He wants life for us and he wants love from us. But in order for us to have that life and give that love, we have to be free to choose it. The tree's existence in the Garden gave Adam and Eve a way of doing that. They could choose God by obeying his command to not eat from the tree. Or they could reject God by disobeying his command. The tree, in other words, gave them the opportunity to exercise their freedom.

The serpent, however, sought to take advantage of this freedom and tempted Adam and Eve by questioning what God had told them and lying to them about the consequences of disobeying God's command:

> The serpent said to the woman, "You will not die. For God knows that when you eat of it your eyes will be opened, and you will be like God, knowing good and evil." (Gen 3:4–5)

Of course, God had already made Adam and Eve in his own likeness and given them many gifts, but Satan tempted them to disbelieve what God had told them and not be satisfied with their limits as creatures.

> So when the woman saw that the tree was good for food, and that it was a delight to the eyes, and that the tree was to be desired to make one wise, she took of its fruit and ate; and she also gave some to her husband, and he ate. (Gen 3:6)

Adam and Eve failed to trust that God had told them the truth. They believed Satan's lie and disobeyed God. In that, they chose themselves and their own will over God and his will (CCC 397–398).

Consequences of Sin

God had warned Adam and Eve that if they were to eat of the fruit of the tree, they would die (Gen 2:17; 3:3). This wasn't simply a threat or a way of intimidating them, but a statement of the true consequences of choosing something other than God.

Sure enough, as soon as Adam and Eve made the choice to disobey God, we immediately see a dramatic change in them. They didn't drop dead on the spot. Physical death didn't come immediately (although that, too, came in time). Instead, they experienced spiritual death. They lost their original holiness and justice. They lost the sanctifying grace—the life of God—that animated their souls. Then, having lost the harmony of original justice within themselves and between each other, they were suddenly ashamed of their nakedness (Gen 3:7). Having broken their friendship with God and believing Satan's lies about him, they ran and hid from him (Gen 3:8). After that, when questioned by God, they pointed fingers at each other instead of taking responsibility for their bad choice (Gen 3:9–12).

God, witnessing all this, foretold that their lives would now be marked by suffering, toil, and, finally, death (Gen 3:16–19). Likewise, because they could not abide by the limits set on them as creatures, they had to leave the garden (Gen 3:22–24). Thus, because of sin, suffering, and death enter human history, and in the following chapters of Genesis, we see the consequences of sin spread throughout the world (CCC 399–401).

This is the world into which we are born—a world of suffering, sin, strife, and death. The sin of our first parents affects us all, and we can't understand our suffering or our tendency to evil apart from this sin (CCC 403). We call the sin of our first parents and the resulting fallen state of human nature that affects every human person "original sin."

This raises an important question: How can it be that everyone, even today, is affected by a sin committed by someone else long ago?

In order to understand the answer to this question, we first need to see that when Genesis tells us that all human beings are descended from a single couple, it teaches us a lesson about the profound unity of the human race. Today, we live in a society that is radically individualistic. It encourages us to see people as isolated individuals who are only responsible for themselves and their actions. But that's not how God made us. He made us as members of closely interconnected communities, where responsibility is shared and the actions of a single person can affect everyone else dramatically. Because the human race is united in this way, when Adam and Eve lost the gifts of original holiness and justice, the entire human race lost them. The human nature that we receive from them as their descendants is deprived of these gifts. St. Paul, reflecting on this, says, "as sin came into the world through one man and death through sin, and so death spread to all men because all men sinned" (Rom 5:12; CCC 404).

That being said, original sin is not "sin" in the sense of a personal sin for which we are guilty. Rather, it refers to this deprived or fallen state. Our nature is not completely corrupted, but it is wounded. We are affected by ignorance, suffering, fear of death, and an inclination toward sin called "concupiscence." This in turn leads to personal sins, for which we are culpable. In this way, sin affects us as individuals and as a society, distorting human social structures, and making us subject in many ways to the power of Satan (CCC 405–408).

The Promise of a Savior

In a sense, original sin is the "bad news": it explains why we are separated from God, why we tend to do what is wrong even when we know better, and why we suffer from conflict, unhappiness, and death. Because of original sin, human life is a battle. We were created in the image of God and meant to enjoy life with him, so we have within us a deep desire for the holiness and justice we lost. At the same time, we are afflicted by sin, its effects, and the power of Satan. As a result, our life is a struggle between competing desires, and we can't overcome that struggle on our own (CCC 409).

Fortunately, God doesn't expect that of us. No sooner did man fall than did God promise to send a savior to rescue us, telling the serpent:

I will put enmity between you and the woman,
and between your seed and her seed;
he shall bruise your head,
and you shall bruise his heel. (Gen 3:15)

In these words, the Church recognizes the first promise of the Savior, Jesus, the descendant of Adam and Eve who would free us from the power of Satan (CCC 410).

SELECTED READING
Pope Benedict XVI, *Papal Audience on Creation*, Part 3 (February 6, 2013)

In the first chapters of the Book of Genesis we find two important images: the garden, with the tree of the knowledge of good and evil, and the serpent (cf. 2:15–17; 3:1–5). The garden tells us that the reality in which God has placed the human being is not a wild forest but a place that protects, nurtures and sustains; and human beings must not consider the world as a property to be looted and exploited but as a gift of the Creator, a sign of his saving will, a gift to be cultivated and safeguarded, to increase and to develop with respect and in harmony, following its rhythms and logic in accordance with God's plan (cf. Gen 2:8–15).

Then the serpent is a symbol that comes from the Oriental fertility cults that fascinated Israel and were a constant temptation to abandon the mysterious covenant with God. In this light Sacred Scripture presents the temptation of Adam and Eve as the core of temptation and sin. What, in fact, did the serpent say? He did not deny God but insinuated a subtle question: "Did God say, 'you shall not eat of any tree of the garden'?" (Gen 3:1). This is how the serpent awoke in them the suspicion that the covenant with God was nothing but a chain that bound them, that deprived them of freedom and of the most beautiful and precious things of life. Their temptation became the temptation to build by themselves the world in which to live, to refuse to accept the limitations of being creatures, the limitations of good and evil, of morality; they saw their dependence on the love of God the Creator as a burden of which to free themselves. This is always the essence of temptation. But when the relationship with God is falsified, with a lie, putting ourselves in his place, all other relationships are altered. The other then becomes a rival, a threat. Straight after succumbing to the temptation, Adam turned on Eve (cf. Gen 3:12); the two conceal themselves from the sight of that God with whom they had been conversing as friends (cf. 3:8–10); the world is no longer the garden in which to live in harmony, but a place to exploit, riddled with hidden snares (cf. 3:14–19); envy and hatred for others entered man's heart. An example of this is Cain who kills his own brother Abel (cf. 4:3–9).

Actually, in opposing their Creator people go against themselves, deny their origin and consequently their truth; and evil, with its painful chain of sorrow and death, enters the world. Moreover, all that God had created was good, indeed, very good, but after man had opted freely for falsehood rather than truth, evil entered the world.

I would like to highlight a final teaching in the accounts of the Creation; sin begets sin and all the sins of history are interconnected. This aspect impels us to speak of what is called "original sin." What is the meaning of this reality that is not easy to understand? I would just like to suggest a few points. First of all we must consider that no human being is closed in on himself, no one can live solely for himself and by himself; we receive life from the other and not only at the moment of our birth but every day. Being human is a relationship: I am myself only in the "you" and through the "you," in the relationship of love with the "you" of God and the "you" of others. Well, sin is the distortion or destruction of the relationship with God, this is its essence: it ruins the relationship with God, the fundamental relationship, by putting ourselves in God's place.

The *Catechism of the Catholic Church* states that with the first sin man "chose himself over and against God, against the requirements of his creaturely status and therefore against his own good" (n. 398). Once the fundamental relationship is spoilt, the other relational poles are also jeopardized or destroyed: sin ruins relationships, thus it ruins everything, because we are relational. Now, if the relationship structure is disordered from the outset, every human being comes into a world marked by this relational distortion, comes into a world disturbed by sin, by which he or she is marked personally; the initial sin tarnishes and wounds human nature (cf. *Catechism of the Catholic Church*, 404–406). And by himself, on his own, man is unable to extricate himself from this situation, on his own he cannot redeem himself; only the Creator himself can right relationships. Only if he from who we distanced ourselves comes to us and lovingly holds out his hand can proper relationships be restored. This happens through Jesus Christ, who goes in exactly the opposite direction to Adam, as is described by the hymn in the second chapter of St Paul's Letter to the Philippians (2:5–11): whereas Adam did not acknowledge his creatural being and wanted to put himself in God's place, Jesus, the Son of God, was in a perfect filial relationship with the Father, he emptied himself and became the servant, he took the path of love, humbling himself even to death on a cross, to set right our relations with God. The Cross of Christ thus became the new tree of life.

Dear brothers and sisters, living out faith means recognizing God's greatness and accepting our smallness, our condition as creatures, letting the Lord fill us with his love and thus develop our true greatness. Evil, with its load of sorrows and sufferings, is a mystery illuminated by the light of faith which gives us the certainty that we can be freed from it: the certainty that it is good to be a human being.

QUESTIONS FOR REVIEW

1. Who is Satan?
2. What did Satan promise Adam and Eve?
3. What did Adam and Eve lose when they disobeyed God?
4. What do we call the sin of our first parents and the fallen state of human nature inherited from them?
5. After announcing their punishment for sin, what good news does God give Adam and Eve?

QUESTIONS FOR DISCUSSION

1. Satan tempted Adam and Eve with a promise that they "could be like God." Today, he continues to tempt people to "play God" and make up a moral law for themselves. Can you think of some examples of people "playing God"? Why is this so dangerous?
2. Because we are all interconnected, both our good and bad actions affect others. Can you think of some examples of how our personal bad choices hurt those around us? What about our good personal choices? How do they help those around us?
3. Because of original sin, we often don't do the good things we know we ought to do. Do you see this tendency in yourself or your friends sometimes? Give one example of this from your personal experience.

Part II

The Promise of a Messiah

As Catholics, we read the Old Testament as a single story—the story of God's unfolding plan for the salvation of humanity, which is fulfilled in Jesus Christ in the New Testament. All the events of the Old Testament are significant because of what they tell us about God and because they are stages in his plan. The people of Israel were entrusted with the keeping of this story of God's promise of salvation until the time of its fulfillment. To them, God promised a Messiah, who would save the people from their sins. God then reached out to the Israelites again and again when they went astray, and he fulfilled his promise by sending his Son, Jesus Christ.

Chapter 1

The First Prophecy of the Messiah

As we saw in Part I, the promise of the Messiah was first revealed after Adam and Eve sinned in the Garden of Eden. God said to the serpent: "I will put enmity between you and the woman, and between your seed and her seed; he shall bruise your head, and you shall bruise his heel" (Gen 3:15).

Since the earliest days of Christianity, this verse has been considered the first announcement of the Good News of Jesus Christ. It's often referred to as the "first gospel" or "protoevangelium"—a first, partial unveiling of God's plan of salvation. As the Catechism puts it:

> After his fall, man was not abandoned by God. On the contrary, God calls him and in a mysterious way heralds the coming victory over evil and his restoration from his fall [Cf. *Gen* 3:9, 15]. (CCC 410)

The word "seed" in this verse means "child" or "descendant." In a general sense, this verse says that the battle between Satan and the human family will continue through the generations. More specifically, tradition has seen the "seed" of the woman as referring to a specific descendant of the woman: Jesus, the promised Messiah.

Sin entered the world through one man—Adam. As the "head" of the human race, Adam lost friendship with God by his disobedience, not just for himself but for the entire human family. At the same time, salvation comes through one man—Jesus. Jesus is the "New Adam," who undoes Adam's disobedience through his perfect obedience and who reunites us to God as the Head of the Body, the Church. St. Paul explains:

> But the free gift is not like the trespass. For if many died through one man's trespass, much more have the grace of God and the free gift in the grace of that one man Jesus Christ abounded for many. And the free gift is not like the effect of that one man's sin. For the judgment following one trespass brought condemnation, but the free gift following many trespasses brings justification. If, because of one man's trespass, death reigned through that one man, much more will those who receive the abundance of grace and the free gift of righteousness reign in life through the one man Jesus Christ. (Rom 5:15–17)

Similarly, as Adam's sin occurred with the help of Eve, Jesus' work of salvation occurs with the cooperation of Mary. Where Eve said "no" to God and then helped lead Adam astray, Mary said "yes" to God and allowed Jesus to enter the world through her. Thus, Mary is called the "New Eve." She is also the first to benefit from Jesus' victory over sin, being preserved by a special grace from original sin and all personal sin (CCC 411).

While the prophecy made in the garden was only fully understood after it was fulfilled in Jesus, we can see that, from the beginning, God shows his power in promising to bring something good out of the evil of our sin. The evil of our sin becomes an opportunity for God to unveil a plan of love and mercy that is greater than our sin and greater even than his original gifts to Adam and Eve (CCC 412).

Before things got better, though, they got worse.

Human Sin and God's Promise

Assigned Reading
Genesis 11:1–9

In the chapters of Genesis that follow, we see the escalation of sin—both in individual lives and in the culture. The escalation starts in Genesis 4, which tells how Adam and Eve's oldest son, Cain, killed his younger brother Abel out of jealousy. Then, when God (already knowing the answer) asks Cain, "Where is Abel your brother?" Cain lies to God and says, "I do not know; am I my brother's keeper?" (Gen 4:9). So, in just one generation, we see sin take the form of jealousy, lying, lack of concern for one's neighbor, and even murder.

This continues for many generations, until the whole world has become so evil that God sends a flood to cleanse the earth of sin, saving only Noah and his family (Gen 6). Even after this, though, the effect of sin on human society continues, and in Genesis 11:1–9, the people at Babel attempt to build a tower that reaches the heavens. This tower is a manifestation of the sin of pride. The people want to "make a name" for themselves apart from God and reach to the heavens on their own.

Nevertheless, despite humanity's persistence in sin, God doesn't give up on us. His promise endures through our sin. He punishes Cain, but protects him (Gen 4:15). He also divides the people at Babel into nations, to limit the damage they can do (Gen 11:6–9). Most significantly, he saves Noah's family from the flood and makes a covenant with him, the first of a series of covenants in the Old Testament, each of which marks a new stage in the unveiling of God's plan and brings us closer to the fulfillment of his promise.

SELECTED READING

Second Vatican Council, Dogmatic Constitution on Divine Revelation *Dei Verbum* (November 18, 1965), nos. 2–6

In His goodness and wisdom God chose to reveal Himself and to make known to us the hidden purpose of His will (see Eph. 1:9) by which through Christ, the Word made flesh, man might in the Holy Spirit have access to the Father and come to share in the divine nature (see Eph. 2:18; 2 Peter 1:4). Through this revelation, therefore, the invisible God (see Col. 1:15, 1 Tim. 1:17) out of the abundance of His love speaks to men as friends (see Ex. 33:11; John 15:14–15) and lives among them (see Bar. 3:38), so that He may invite and take them into fellowship with Himself. This plan of revelation is realized by deeds and words having an inner unity: the deeds wrought by God in the history of salvation manifest and confirm the teaching and realities signified by the words, while the words proclaim the deeds and clarify the mystery contained in them. By this revelation then, the deepest truth about God and the salvation of man shines out for our sake in Christ, who is both the mediator and the fullness of all revelation.

God, who through the Word creates all things (see John 1:3) and keeps them in existence, gives men an enduring witness to Himself in created realities (see Rom. 1:19–20). Planning to make known the way of heavenly salvation, He went further and from the start manifested Himself to our first parents. Then after their fall His promise of redemption aroused in them the hope of being saved (see Gen. 3:15) and from that time on He ceaselessly kept the human race in His care, to give eternal life to those who perseveringly do good in search of salvation (see Rom. 2:6–7). Then, at the time He had appointed He called Abraham in order to make of him a great nation (see Gen. 12:2). Through the patriarchs, and after them through Moses and the prophets, He taught this people to acknowledge Himself the one living and true God, provident father and just judge, and to wait for the Savior promised by Him, and in this manner prepared the way for the Gospel down through the centuries.

Then, after speaking in many and varied ways through the prophets, "now at last in these days God has spoken to us in His Son" (Heb. 1:1–2). For He sent His Son, the eternal Word, who enlightens all men, so that He might dwell among men and tell them of the innermost being of God (see John 1:1–18). Jesus Christ, therefore, the Word made flesh, was sent as "a man to men." He "speaks the words of God" (John 3; 34), and completes the work of salvation which His Father gave Him to do (see John 5:36; John 17:4). To see Jesus is to see His Father (John 14:9). For this reason Jesus perfected revelation by fulfilling it through his whole work of making Himself present and manifesting Himself: through His words and deeds, His signs and wonders, but especially through His death and glorious resurrection from the dead and final sending of the Spirit of truth. Moreover He confirmed with divine testimony what revelation proclaimed, that God is with us to free us from the darkness of sin and death, and to raise us up to life eternal.

The Christian dispensation, therefore, as the new and definitive covenant, will never pass away and we now await no further new public revelation before the glorious manifestation of our Lord Jesus Christ (see 1 Tim. 6:14 and Tit. 2:13). "The obedience of faith" (Rom. 16:26; see 1:5; 2 Cor 10:5–6) "is to be given to God who reveals, an obedience by which man commits his whole self freely to God, offering the full submission of intellect and will to God who reveals," and freely assenting to the truth revealed by Him. To make this act of faith, the grace of God and the interior help of the Holy Spirit must precede and assist, moving the heart and turning it to God, opening the eyes of the mind and giving "joy and ease to everyone in assenting to the truth and believing it." To bring about an ever deeper understanding of revelation the same Holy Spirit constantly brings faith to completion by His gifts.

Through divine revelation, God chose to show forth and communicate Himself and the eternal decisions of His will regarding the salvation of men. That is to say, He chose to share with them those divine treasures which totally transcend the understanding of the human mind.

QUESTIONS FOR REVIEW

1. What is the "protoevangelium"?
2. Why does the Church call Jesus the "New Adam"?
3. Why does the Church call Mary the "New Eve"?
4. What is the first way we see sin escalate after the fall of Adam and Eve?
5. What did the Tower of Babel symbolize?

QUESTIONS FOR DISCUSSION

1. From the beginning, God has brought good out of sorrow. Have you ever experienced God bringing something good out of a bad situation in your life? Describe.
2. Great good came into the world because Jesus and Mary cooperated with God's plan for our redemption. They said yes to him. What is one way you can say yes to God today?
3. After Adam and Eve fell, their sin quickly escalated. Have you ever seen one sin lead to another, and then another? Describe.

Chapter 2

Longing for the Fulfillment of the Promise

The Old Testament: God Reveals His Plan in History

The Old Testament is an indispensable part of salvation history. It is the record of God's dealings with humanity in preparation for his full revelation of himself in his Son, Jesus Christ. It also is the record of humanity's longing for redemption and God's slowly unfolding plan to fulfill this longing in Jesus. Not only does it contain great wisdom about God and human life in its own right, but it also contains hints and promises about the Messiah to come, helping us to better understand the life and mission of Jesus (CCC 121–123).

In the Old Testament, those hints and promises come to us largely through a series of covenants, or solemn, family-making commitments, that God makes with human beings. Sin had separated human beings from God and had destroyed the unity of the human race, but God responded by seeking out individuals and groups of people and uniting them to himself by forming covenants with them (CCC 56).

When we read the history of these covenants in the light of the New Testament, we see them pointing toward and foreshadowing Jesus. At the same time, the covenants of the Old Testament are important in their own right, both for the relationship they establish between God and human beings, and because they serve as stages in preparation for the coming of Jesus (CCC 129–130).

Noah

> **Assigned Reading**
> Genesis 8:20–9:17

After the Fall and the escalation of sin that followed, God reaches out to form a covenant with Noah. The story of the great flood and the ark of Noah in Genesis 6:5–9:17 is one of the most famous in the Old Testament. Even though the earth was filled with violence and corruption, to the point that God regretted creating man, the earth still contained one righteous man: Noah. Noah found favor in God's eyes and "walked with God" (Gen 6:9), so God chose to "reset" the world through Noah and his family. To do so, God told Noah to build an ark and take upon it two of every kind of animal. Then, once the ark was packed, God let rain fall upon the earth for forty days and forty nights. At the end, Noah, his family, and the animals they had gathered onto the ark were the only living beings that survived.

After the waters receded and his family disembarked onto dry land, Noah offered a sacrifice to God. Sacrifice—offering something valuable back to God as a sign of worship, thanksgiving, or in atonement for sin—has been practiced in some form by most human cultures and religions. Sacrifice expresses the fact that everything we have belongs to God and that we depend upon him and trust in him rather than in our own power and wealth.

God was pleased with Noah's sacrifice and resolved to never again send destruction like he did with the flood (Gen 8:21–22). He then blessed Noah and his sons, and as he did with Adam and Eve, he commanded them to be fruitful and fill the earth. He also gave them permission to eat the fruits of creation, but this time, unlike with Adam and Eve, in addition to plants, God also gave them permission to eat meat. He forbade them, however, from eating the blood of animals—because blood is seen as sacred and bearing life—and established a punishment for anyone who shed the blood of another person (Gen 9:1–7).

After this, God made a promise with Noah, his descendants, and every living creature:

> Behold, I establish my covenant with you and your descendants after you, and with every living creature that is with you, the birds, the cattle, and every beast of the earth with you, as many as came out of the ark. I establish my covenant with you, that never again shall all flesh be cut off by the waters of a flood, and never again shall there be a flood to destroy the earth. (Gen 9:9–11)

Finally, he set the rainbow in the sky as the sign of this covenant (Gen 9:12–13).

Following the flood, Genesis explains how all the nations of the earth are descended from Noah and his sons. Accordingly, God's covenant with Noah applies to all Noah's descendants—that is, all the nations of the earth, "for all future generations" (Gen 9:12). While the rest of the Old Testament mainly concerns the particular covenants God made with his people Israel, the covenant of Noah remains in force for all the non-Jewish peoples (often called the "Gentiles" in the Bible) until the universal proclamation of the Gospel (CCC 56–58).

Abraham

Assigned Reading
Genesis 17:1–27

The nations are scattered after the destruction of the Tower of Babel (Gen 11), but God's plan to gather them together again begins to unfold with a single man—Abram. At the end of Genesis 11, God called Abram to leave his home country and go to the land of Canaan. In return, God made three promises to Abram: (1) he promised to bless Abram with a great number of descendants; (2) he promised to make a great nation out of those descendants; and (3) he promised Abram that blessing would come to all the earth through him. Like Noah, Abram trusted God and obeyed him, traveling to the land of Canaan and offering sacrifice to God there (Gen 12:1–9). After this, God strengthened his promises by making a covenant with Abram and instituting circumcision as a sign of this covenant.

God also changed Abram's name to Abraham, which means "father of a multitude of nations." Even though Abraham and his wife were too old to have children, God swore that nations and kings would descend from him, and he promised to establish his covenant with Abraham's descendants as well. Soon after, in their old age, the couple conceived a son: Isaac. Isaac in turn had a son, Jacob, who was later given the name "Israel." The families of Jacob's twelve sons became the twelve tribes of the nation of Israel: God's chosen people. To them God entrusted his promise of salvation, and from them God raised up the promised savior, through whom all the nations are blessed (CCC 60).

Moses

> **Assigned Reading**
> Exodus 19:1–9

At the end of Genesis, Jacob and his sons left Canaan and went to Egypt to escape a famine. In Egypt, their descendants multiplied greatly over several generations, and the Egyptians, out of fear, eventually enslaved them. The next book of the Bible, Exodus, recalls how God raised up Moses to lead his people out of slavery.

To bring this about, God intervened dramatically, convincing Pharaoh to release Israel by sending a series of ten plagues upon Egypt (Exod 7:14–12:32). The final plague killed the firstborn children and livestock of Egypt, but the Jews escaped it by observing the first Passover meal—where each household sacrificed a lamb and put its blood on the doorposts of their home (Exod 12:1–28). After this, Pharaoh relented and told the Israelites they were free to leave. No sooner did they escape into the desert, however, than did Pharaoh change his mind. With his army, he set off in pursuit, only to be thwarted by God, who parted the

Red Sea so Israel could pass through and then brought the waters crashing back down on Pharaoh's army (Exod 14).

When Israel, safe at last, reached Mount Sinai, God formed a covenant with them through Moses. There, God gave Israel the Law to help form them as his people. At the center of the Law is the "Decalogue," better known as the Ten Commandments (Exod 20:1–21). The Law describes in detail how Israel was to be governed and how they were to worship God. After giving them the Law, God promised that if Israel obeyed him and kept his covenant, they would be his own possession among all the peoples of the world, "a kingdom of priests and a holy nation" (Exod 19:5–6). The Catechism explains:

> God formed Israel as his people by freeing them from slavery in Egypt. He established with them the covenant of Mount Sinai and, through Moses, gave them his law so that they would recognize him and serve him as the one living and true God, the provident Father and just judge, and so that they would look for the promised Savior [Cf. *DV* 3]. (CCC 62)

Foreshadowing the Paschal Mystery

The covenants of the Old Testament all point to the New Covenant established by God in Jesus. As man, Jesus obeyed the Father perfectly, fulfilling the requirements of the covenants, and, as God, he himself is the perfect fulfillment of God's promises in the Old Testament to save us and dwell with us.

When we read the Old Testament covenants in light of their fulfillment in Jesus, we see how they foreshadow Jesus and his Paschal Mystery. In the people, events, and signs of the Old Testament covenants, we see symbols, called "types," which point to elements of the New Covenant (CCC 129). For example, the First Letter of Saint Peter explains how the flood prefigures Baptism:

> God's patience waited in the days of Noah, during the building of the ark, in which a few, that is, eight persons, were saved through

> water. Baptism, which corresponds to this, now saves you, not as a removal of dirt from the body but as an appeal to God for a clear conscience, through the resurrection of Jesus Christ, who has gone into heaven and is at the right hand of God, with angels, authorities, and powers subject to him. (1 Pet 3:20–22)

The flood cleansed humanity from sin so that Noah and his descendants could enter into a covenant with God. In the same way, Baptism washes us from sin through the power of Jesus' Resurrection so that we can enter into the New Covenant.

Likewise, in the covenant of Abraham, circumcision is the sign by which Abraham and his descendants enter the covenant, and it, too, prefigures Baptism. Even in the Old Testament, circumcision is an outward sign that is supposed to reflect an inward change (Deut 10:16; 30:6; Jer 4:4). This circumcision of the heart is brought about by Jesus and is accomplished sacramentally in Baptism, by which we enter the New Covenant (Col 2:11–13). Similarly, God's promises to Abraham find their ultimate fulfillment in Jesus. Abraham is a father not just of Israel but of a "multitude of nations" (Gen 17:5), because he is the father of all believers. Not only are the kings of Israel descended from Abraham (Gen 17:6), but Jesus, the King of kings, is descended from him (Rev 19:16). And because of Jesus, all nations are blessed through Abraham (Gen 12:3; 22:18; Gal 3:8).

There are many other elements in the story of the Exodus and the covenant of Sinai that point to Jesus and find their fulfillment in him. As in the flood, at the Red Sea God's people are delivered through water, and this prefigures Baptism (1 Cor 10:1–4). Moses gives the Law from Mount Sinai as Jesus gives his New Law from a mountain (Matt 5:1). And the Law forms Israel into a nation centered on the worship of God. This prefigures the Church.

Most of all, Christ and his saving death and Resurrection are prefigured in the Passover (or "Pasch"). In the first Passover, God delivered Israel from slavery and death through the blood of an unblemished lamb. He then established the Passover meal as an annual commemoration of this event. In the New Testament, when Jesus went to Jerusalem to celebrate the Passover with his disciples, he fulfilled the law completely by becoming the true unblemished "Lamb of God, who takes away the sin of the world" (John 1:29). He delivered us from the slavery of sin and death by shedding his blood on the Cross, and he established the Eucharist as the memorial of this new Passover—which we refer to as the "Paschal Mystery."

The Promise Entrusted to Israel

The people of ancient Israel, formed by the covenant of Sinai, were entrusted with the knowledge of God's promise to send a Messiah. And just as God foreshadowed the mystery of salvation through the covenants with Noah, Abraham, and Moses, he continued to prepare the way for Jesus through the history of Israel. In the judges, kings, and prophets of the Old Testament, we can see how the meaning of the promise and the identity of the savior was revealed and became clearer over time.

The Judges

After wandering for forty years in the desert, Israel entered the Promised Land. There, in the midst of other nations who worshipped other gods, they struggled to remain faithful to the one true God. In the Book of Judges, we read about how God helped them overcome those temptations by raising up particular individuals, called "judges," to bring Israel back when they strayed. He didn't just do this once, but many, many times. Whenever Israel would sin and start worshipping other gods, they would be defeated and plundered by their enemies. Then God would be merciful and send a judge to rescue his people. The judge would remind Israel of the covenant and God's promises and then lead them to victory over their enemies. In this way, God's faithfulness and mercy kept alive the promise of salvation despite Israel's sins and prepared the way for Jesus, who, like the judges, called us back to God and won the victory over sin and death.

The Kings

After the time of the judges, the Books of Samuel tell how Israel became a kingdom under Saul and David. When the Israelites first requested a king, God warned them that this would lead to their oppression (1 Sam 8:1–18). This, however, didn't dissuade them. They wanted to be like other nations, ruled not by God but by a man. So, God let them have their way. The first king he had the prophet Samuel appoint, Saul, fell from power after he disobeyed God. The next king God chose, however, was a righteous man, who sought to honor God. His name was David. God was pleased with David and greatly blessed him and all Israel during his reign. God also promised David that a descendant of his would sit on his throne forever:

> When your days are fulfilled and you lie down with your fathers, I will raise up your offspring after you, who shall come forth from your body, and I will establish his kingdom. He shall build a house for my name, and I will establish the throne of his kingdom for ever. (2 Sam 7:12–14)

Unfortunately, the kings that followed David didn't follow in his footsteps, and God's warnings of Israel's suffering under bad kings came true. The Books of Kings tell how the kingdom fell into sin after David. The kings worshipped other gods and heavily taxed their people, until eventually the people rebelled and the kingdom split into two. After that, the Kingdom of Israel in the north was centered in Samaria. The Kingdom of Judah in the south was centered in Jerusalem and was ruled by the descendants of David. The two kingdoms wandered further and further from God, until they were eventually conquered—the Northern Kingdom by Assyria and the Southern Kingdom by Babylon. With the fall of the two kingdoms, all the Israelites were sent into exile, the descendants of David no longer ruled in Jerusalem, and the Temple built for God by David's son Solomon was destroyed.

The Prophets

> **Assigned Reading**
> Isaiah 52:13–53:12

As in the time of the judges, when the kings and people strayed from God, they suffered from their enemies because of their sins, but God still reached out to them again and again through the prophets. At first, the prophets called the sinful kings and all the people to repentance from idolatry, oppression, and other sins against the covenant with God. They warned them of the ruin coming upon them because of their lack of faithfulness. Then, when ruin came, the prophets helped people see that God had not abandoned them or forgotten his promises.

In fact, the prophets foretold, not only would God end their exile and rebuild Jerusalem and the Temple, but he would bring about a more far-reaching redemption: a new covenant and a new law written not on stone but upon human hearts (Jer 31:33). In this new covenant, all nations would turn to the God of Israel (Isa 2:2–4) and the promise God made to David—that a descendant of David, a "prince of peace," would reign forever (Isa 9:6–7)—would be fulfilled. This prince of peace would be the Messiah, a word which means "anointed one" (CCC 64).

Of all the prophets, Isaiah probably gives the most information about the promised savior, but he doesn't depict him only as a triumphant king. Rather, in a series of songs he describes the savior as the servant of the Lord, who is chosen by God, anointed by the Spirit, sent to bring justice to the nations (Isa 42:1) and save the people from their sins.

Isaiah further prophesied that the Servant of the Lord would save us not as a military conqueror but by suffering in our place for our sins (Isa 53:5), like a lamb that is taken to be slaughtered (Isa 53:7). Even though he would be innocent, he would give himself as a sacrifice for our sins, be stricken, cut off from the land of the living, and receive a grave with the wicked (Isa 53:8–9). In the end, though, Isaiah foretold, God would make him live and triumph (Isa 53:10–11).

This prophecy is ultimately fulfilled in the Paschal Mystery of Jesus.

SELECTED READING

Jeff Cavins, "His Story Is Your Story," in *Catholic for a Reason III: Scripture and the Mystery of the Family of God*, pp. 29–30

The Bible, although made up of many stories, contains a single story within its pages. Though not evident at first glance, the story is about God and His relationship with His creation, the universe. As the Creator of the universe, God could certainly have said much about the beauty and complexity of the galaxies. However, He limits the field on which this divine story is played out primarily to planet Earth. While the Earth is marvelous and in itself speaks of His power and glory, its role is to be a glorious stage for the greatest story ever told.

At center stage stands man, the most complex creation in the universe and the true object of God's love and affection. Man would betray God, and yet God in turn would die for man, and by means of a covenant bring man into the family life of the Trinity. This is the world's story, invented, orchestrated, and executed by God. By inviting us to be His friends, companions, and, most importantly, His sons and daughters, Our Heavenly Father has made His story our story.

From the very beginning, it was God's intention to walk with mankind in a love relationship, but this relationship was severed through the disobedience of Adam and Eve. The fall of Adam and Eve introduced sin into the human race and has had devastating repercussions down through the centuries. Out of balance with his Maker, yet with the desire for God written in his heart (cf. *Catechism*, no. 27), man struggles to find meaning in life.

Starting with the very early chapters of Genesis all the way through the Book of Revelation, God gradually reveals His plan to reestablish the broken relationship between Himself and His treasured creation. Only in God's revealed plan does man once again find his intended purpose for being, "because man is created by God and for God; and God never ceases to draw man to himself. Only in God will he find the truth and happiness he never stops searching for" (*Catechism*, no. 27).

It is important for all Catholics to understand that, when they read the Bible, they are reading a book of history. History is very important to the Christian, for God has revealed Himself through actual human events. There should be no misunderstanding—this is actual history as opposed to cleverly devised tales. Pope Paul VI said, "The history of salvation is being accomplished in the midst of the history of the world." The Bible provides countless examples of how, through word and deed, God has entered the life of His people.

Although God greatly loves all of mankind, we see early on in the Scriptures that His strategy to redeem humanity was to start with one family, Noah's, and then progressively unite more and more people until all of mankind would have the opportunity to be a part of His worldwide family. Interwoven throughout the family story is a divine method of teaching. The divine plan of Revelation

> is realized by deeds and words, which are intrinsically bound up with each other. As a result, the works performed by God in the history of salvation show forth and bear out the doctrine and realities signified by the words; the words, for their part, proclaim the works, and bring to light the mystery they contain. (DV 2)

God communicates Himself to us gradually by this method so as to welcome us in stages. The Bible narrates the mighty deeds of God as they relate to the salvation of man. These great deeds of God are understood in and through the lesser deeds of the various biblical characters. For example, the sacrificial nature of God's love is graphically illustrated and better understood in the story of Abraham's nearly sacrificing his son Isaac, found in Gen. 22. In this passage, we learn one of the revelatory names of God, *Yahweh Jireh*, "the Lord will provide" (Gen. 22:14).

Dei Verbum speaks of this gradual self-communication of God:

> [W]ishing to open up the way to heavenly salvation, he manifested himself to our first parents from the very beginning. After the fall, he buoyed them up with the hope of salvation, by promising redemption (cf. Gen. 3:15); and he has never ceased to take care of the human race. For he wishes to give eternal life to all those who seek salvation by patience in well-doing (cf. Rom. 2:6–7). In his own time God called Abraham, and made him into a great nation (cf. Gen. 12:2). After the era of the patriarchs, he taught this nation, by Moses and the prophets, to recognize him as the only living and true God, as a provident Father and just judge. He taught them, too, to look for the promised Saviour. And so, throughout the ages, he prepared the way for the Gospel.
>
> After God had spoken many times and in various ways through the prophets, "in these last days he has spoken to us by a Son" (Heb. 1:1–2). For he sent his Son, the eternal Word who enlightens all men. (DV 3–4)

QUESTIONS FOR REVIEW

1. What are covenants?
2. What does a sacrifice offered to God express?
3. Name three figures from the Old Testament with whom God made covenants.
4. What was the role of the Judges in ancient Israel?
5. Name two ways Baptism was prefigured in the Old Covenant.

QUESTIONS FOR DISCUSSION

1. How would you describe God's dealings with Israel? Do you think he was patient? Persistent? Something else? Why?
2. Has God ever been patient and persistent with you? If so, how?
3. God worked hard to prepare Israel to receive the Messiah. How has God prepared you for the tasks and trials you're currently facing?

Chapter 3

The Promise Fulfilled

All the foreshadowing, prophecies, and anxious waiting found in the Old Testament are illuminated by the Gospel account of the life of Jesus.

The Gospels Recognize Jesus as the Fulfillment of the Promise

In the fullness of time, when all things had been prepared and the people of Israel made ready, God sent the angel Gabriel to a virgin named Mary in the small town of Nazareth to announce to her that she would conceive and bear a son:

> And the angel said to her, "Do not be afraid, Mary, for you have found favor with God. And behold, you will conceive in your womb and bear a son, and you shall call his name Jesus. He will be great, and will be called the Son of the Most High; and the Lord God will give to him the throne of his father David, and he will reign over the house of Jacob for ever; and of his kingdom there will be no end." (Luke 1:30–33)

Mary asks how this can be, since she is a virgin, and Gabriel tells her that she will conceive by the power of the Holy Spirit, and therefore the child will be holy, the Son of God (Luke 1:34–35).

Mary responds, saying, "Behold, I am the handmaid of the Lord; let it be to me according to your word" (Luke 1:38). In Course 2, we learned how God made Mary "full of grace," free from all sin so that she could bring Jesus into the world. By trusting God and saying yes, Mary undoes the untrusting no of Eve. As St. Irenaeus (ca. 130–202) wrote:

> The knot of Eve's disobedience was loosed by the obedience of Mary. For what the virgin Eve had bound fast through unbelief, this did the virgin Mary set free through faith.[1]

God built up Israel to bring Christ to the world, and Mary is the particular representative of Israel through whom he comes. She is the "God Bearer," the *Theotokos*, or "Mother of God." In this role, she comes at the end of a long line of holy women who prepared the way for the savior (CCC 489).

Although God, and not any human man, is Jesus' father, Mary didn't have to raise Jesus alone. At the time the angel came to her, she was betrothed to a man named Joseph. The Gospels don't tell us much about St. Joseph, but he played an important role in the life of Jesus and Mary. St. Matthew's Gospel tells how, like Mary, Joseph was told about Jesus by an angel:

> When his mother Mary had been betrothed to Joseph, before they came together she was found to be with child of the Holy Spirit; and her husband Joseph, being a just man and unwilling to put her to shame, resolved to send her away quietly. But as he considered this, behold, an angel of the Lord appeared to him in a dream, saying, "Joseph, son of David, do not fear to take Mary your wife, for that which is conceived in her is of the Holy Spirit;

---

[1] Irenaeus of Lyons, *Irenæus against Heresies* 3.22.4, in *The Apostolic Fathers with Justin Martyr and Irenaeus*, ed. Alexander Roberts, James Donaldson, and A. Cleveland Coxe, The Ante-Nicene Fathers (Buffalo, NY: Christian Literature Company, 1885), 1:455.

> she will bear a son, and you shall call his name Jesus, for he will save his people from their sins." (Matt 1:18–21)

Like Mary, Joseph trusted in God and helped prepare the way for Jesus, accepting the role of foster father (CCC 496–498), living with Mary (who remained a virgin all her life) in perfect chastity, sharing in her holy mission, and completely dedicating himself to Jesus.

Significantly, the angel addresses Joseph as "son of David." Even though he is only Jesus' foster father, because he is the head of the household, the genealogy of Jesus is traced through him (Matt 1:1–17; Luke 3:23–38). So it is through Joseph that Jesus is a member of the house of David.

After the angel speaks to him, Joseph takes Mary to Bethlehem, the city of David, where Jesus is born, and the Gospels show Joseph protecting Mary and Jesus throughout Jesus' childhood. Later, he trusts God again when an angel warns him to flee to Egypt to escape Herod (Matt 2:13–18), and then again when another angel tells him to return to Nazareth after Herod has died (Matt 2:19–23).

Jesus Fulfills the Ancient Prophecies

Conceived by the power of Holy Spirit, Jesus is the "Christ" (literally, the anointed one), the Messiah who has been anointed by the Holy Spirit to save God's people (Isa 61:1; Luke 4:18; Acts 10:38; CCC 486). Throughout the Gospels we see how Jesus fulfills the prophecies about the Messiah found in the Old Testament. The sacred writers in fact often point this out explicitly, saying that a particular event in the life of Jesus occurred in order to fulfill something written in the Old Testament. The following table gives some examples.

Gospel Verse	OT Verse	OT Prophecy	Fulfillment
Matt 1:22–23	Isa 7:14	"a virgin shall conceive and bear a son."	Jesus was born of a virgin.
Matt 2:15	Hos 11:1	"Out of Egypt have I called my son."	Jesus, Mary, and Joseph escaped to Egypt and then were called back to Israel.
Matt 4:14–16	Isa 9:1–2	"The land of Zeb'ulun and the land of Naph'tali . . . the people who sat in darkness have seen a great light."	Jesus lived in the region of Zeb'ulun and Naph'tali.
Matt 8:17	Isa 53:4	"He took our infirmities and bore our diseases."	Jesus cured the sick.
Matt 12:17–20	Isa 42:1–4	"He will not wrangle or cry aloud."	Jesus told people not to make him known before the appointed time.
Matt 13:35	Ps 78:2	"I will open my mouth in parables."	Jesus taught in parables.
Matt 21:4–5	Isa 62:11; Zech 9:9	"Behold, your king is coming to you, humble, and mounted on a donkey."	Jesus rode into Jerusalem on an ass.
John 12:37–41	Isa 53:1; 6:9–10	"He has blinded their eyes and hardened their heart."	Many did not believe in Jesus.
John 13:18	Ps 41:9	"He who ate my bread has lifted his heel against me."	Judas shared in the Last Supper, then betrayed Jesus.

Gospel Verse	OT Verse	OT Prophecy	Fulfillment
John 15:25	Ps 35:19	"They hated me without a cause."	Many reacted to Jesus with hatred.
John 19:23–34	Ps 22:18	"They parted my garments among them."	The soldiers divided Jesus' garments at the Crucifixion.
John 19:36	Exod 12:46	"Not a bone of him shall be broken."	The soldiers did not break Jesus' legs.
John 19:37	Zech 12:10	"They shall look on him whom they have pierced."	Jesus' side was pierced.

While some of these seem like small details, they illustrate how the sacred authors see everything in the Old Testament as pointing to and prefiguring Jesus (CCC 522). Taken together with the larger story of Jesus' life, they show how Jesus fulfills the portraits of the Messiah given in the Old Testament.

For example, at the beginning of his Gospel, Matthew identifies Jesus as the "Christ" (the Greek word for Messiah) and the "son of David, the son of Abraham" (Matt 1:1). He then traces Jesus' genealogy all the way from Abraham through David to Jesus. Jesus is the descendant of Abraham in whom the nations are blessed (Gen 12:3; 22:18; Gal 3:8), and the son of David, the King of Kings, who fulfills the promise made to David (2 Sam 7:12–14). As foretold in the Old Testament, he is born of a virgin (Matt 1:23; Isa 7:14) in Bethlehem (Matt 2:5–6; Mic 5:2).

The public ministry of Jesus is preceded by the preaching of John the Baptist, who is "the voice of one crying in the wilderness" foretold by Isaiah (Isa 40:3). As the last of the prophets pointing to Jesus, John fulfills the mission of Elijah foretold by Malachi (Matt 11:14; 17:10–13; Mal 4:5; CCC 523).

Jesus himself applies the prophecies of the Old Testament to himself and, in Luke 4:16–19, reads aloud the prophecy in Isaiah 61:1–2 about the mission of the Messiah:

> The Spirit of the Lord is upon me,
> because he has anointed me to preach good news to the poor.
> He has sent me to proclaim release to the captives
> and recovering of sight to the blind,
> to set at liberty those who are oppressed,
> to proclaim the acceptable year of the Lord.

Then, Jesus tells the people, "Today this Scripture has been fulfilled in your hearing" (Luke 4:21). Likewise, when the disciples of John ask Jesus if he is the Messiah, Jesus responds, "Go and tell John what you hear and see: the blind receive their sight and the lame walk, lepers are cleansed and the deaf hear, and the dead are raised up, and the poor have good news preached to them" (Matt 11:4–5). These are the signs of the Messiah's coming named by Isaiah (Isa 26:19; 29:18–19; 35:5–6; 61:1).

Above all, Jesus fulfills the Old Testament through his death and Resurrection. His perfect obedience undoes the disobedience of Adam and Eve and perfectly fulfills the requirements of the Law of Moses. He is the Suffering Servant of the Lord, who "was wounded for our transgressions" (Isa 53:5) but was raised up by the Lord. He is the true Passover Lamb, who takes away the sins of the world and delivers us from death (John 1:29).

Why the Word Became Flesh

Through Jesus, God fulfilled his promise of a savior in a way beyond what anyone at the time expected or imagined. Jesus, the Savior, is God's own Son. He is fully God and fully man, the Word made flesh (John 1:14). This is the mystery of the Incarnation, the central truth of our faith.

The Nicene Creed we recite at Mass every Sunday explains the purpose of the Incarnation: the Son of God "came down from heaven for us men and our salvation." His mission, simply put, is the salvation of humanity. Understanding the "why" behind that mission is a bit more complicated. God's generosity in the mystery of the Incarnation and our salvation is greater than we can fully comprehend. It's impossible for us to fully grasp the love that led God to give such a gift. That being said, there are certain things we can know.

First, we know that the Word became flesh to save us from our sins, thereby reconciling us with God (CCC 457). Through many long centuries, the Israelites offered sacrifices to atone for their sins. But, no matter how many sacrifices they offered, it wasn't enough. It couldn't be enough. What was the blood of lambs and doves compared to all the damage brought about by humanity's sins? Jesus' sacrifice, however, was different. He was truly man, so he could serve as a representative for the whole human race, just as Adam did. But he was also God, so his sacrifice could be perfect. His obedience could be perfect. His love could be perfect. As both God and man, Jesus unites, in himself, our human nature with his divine nature, so his suffering and death on the Cross in perfect obedience to the Father truly delivered us from death. It truly redeemed us from slavery to sin. He paid the price we couldn't pay and, in the process, reunited us with God. Jesus, fully human and fully divine, is the unique mediator between God and man, bridging the division opened up by sin.

Second, we know that the Word became flesh to destroy the power of the devil. As St. John tells us, "The reason the Son of God appeared was to destroy the works of the devil" (1 John 3:8). Sin makes us subject to the power of Satan, but by liberating us from sin, Jesus overcame the power that Satan has over us. Before Jesus began his public ministry, he was tempted by the devil, but unlike Adam and Eve, Jesus was victorious; he didn't give into temptation. Remember, Satan is not equal in power to God. As a fallen angel, Satan is powerful, but only God is all-powerful. God shows his decisive power over Satan in Christ, and followers of Christ can turn to his power to deliver them from the power and temptation of Satan.

Third, we know the Word became flesh to show us the depth of God's love for us. Jesus, remember, is the ultimate revelation of God to us (CCC 458). From him, we learn who God is. And what we learn is that "God is love" (1 John 4:8); he is a communion of divine Persons—the Trinity—united in love.

More specifically, through Jesus we know that God the Father sent his Son to save us: "In this the love of God was made manifest among us, that God sent his only-begotten Son into the world, so that we might live through him" (1 John 4:9). Likewise, Jesus shows the depths of this love by giving his life for his Church: "Christ loved the Church and gave himself up for her, that he might sanctify her, having cleansed her by the washing of water with the word, that he might present the church to himself in splendor, without spot or wrinkle or any such thing, that she might be holy and without blemish" (Eph 5:25–27). Lastly, through Jesus we know the Holy Spirit, whom St. Augustine described as the love between the Father and the Son.[2] The Holy Spirit is God's gift to his people, at work in the Church and in the hearts of individual believers, sanctifying us and making us fruitful: "God's love has been poured into our hearts through the Holy Spirit who has been given to us" (Rom 5:5).

In all these ways, Jesus revealed that God is love. He demonstrated the depth of God's love for us by becoming man, sharing our life, and giving his life for us on the Cross, and he continues to enable us to share in that love.

Another thing we know about the Incarnation is that Jesus became man in order to show us how to be holy. In that, he reveals to us what it means to be fully human (see Course 2, Part IV). He does this, in part, by giving us a New Law, the Law of the Gospel, which teaches us how to grow in holiness and goodness. We find this teaching in the Gospels, especially the Sermon on the Mount in Matthew 5–7. Jesus likewise summarizes it in the two greatest commandments:

> The first is, "Hear, O Israel: The Lord our God, the Lord is one; and you shall love the Lord your God with all your heart, and with all your soul, and with all your mind, and with all your strength." The second is this, "You shall love your neighbor as yourself." There is no other commandment greater than these. (Mark 12:29–31)

---

[2] Augustine of Hippo, *On the Trinity* 6.5.7, in *St. Augustin: On the Holy Trinity, Doctrinal Treatises, Moral Treatises, ed. Philip Schaff*, trans. Arthur West Haddan, A Select Library of the Nicene and Post-Nicene Fathers of the Christian Church, First Series (Buffalo, NY: Christian Literature Company, 1887), 3:100.

The Law of the Gospel is love, and Jesus himself perfectly fulfills this law. He is our model for how to love:

> This is my commandment, that you love one another as I have loved you. Greater love has no man than this, that a man lay down his life for his friends. You are my friends if you do what I command you. (John 15:12–14)

Jesus didn't just tell people how to act, though; he led by example, caring for the sick, the outcast, and the sinner, and ultimately, going to the Cross for love of us. In this, too, God asks us to follow Jesus' example: "If any man would come after me, let him deny himself and take up his cross and follow me" (Mark 8:34).

Finally, we know that Jesus took on flesh in order to make us sharers in the divine nature. Jesus not only overcomes the division between God and man created by sin, but gives us an even deeper kind of communion with God than what Adam and Eve had before the Fall. In the Incarnation, the Son of God unites his divine nature with our human nature. He shares in every aspect of our human life so that we can share in his divine life. The Son of God became a human being so that human beings could be adopted as sons and daughters of God. As St. Irenaeus said:

> For this is why the Word became man, and the Son of God became the Son of man: so that man, by entering into communion with the Word and thus receiving divine sonship, might become a son of God.[3]

This doesn't mean that we become God himself or that we cease to be human, but rather that by sharing in the life of Jesus—who is both God and man—we become so intimately united to God that we share in his life, like a husband and wife share their lives. Or, to use another analogy, through Jesus, the Son, we become sons and daughters of God, sharing in the life of the Holy Trinity like children share in the life of their family.

---

[3] Irenaeus, *Against Heresies* 3.9.1.

In Eastern Christian theology this process is called *theosis* (or "divinization"). It recognizes that the more we unite ourselves to Christ and become like him—through the sacraments and by following his teachings—the more we participate in the inner life of the Holy Trinity.

Christ's Whole Life Is a Mystery of Redemption

The Son of God came down from heaven for our salvation. His mission was our salvation, and so his entire life is a mystery that redeems every aspect of human life (CCC 517).

First, his poverty enriched our poverty. As God, Jesus is rich in power and glory, but by taking on our human nature, he became poor:

> . . . though he was in the form of God, [Jesus] did not count equality with God a thing to be grasped, but emptied himself, taking the form of a servant, being born in the likeness of men. And being found in human form he humbled himself and became obedient unto death, even death on a cross. (Phil 2:6–7)

Not only did Jesus enter in the relative poverty of our human nature, he took on the life of the truly poor and suffering—from coming to this world as a poor child born in a stable to leaving it (temporarily) as a condemned man who suffered the most shameful kind of execution. He didn't just occasionally minister to the sick, the needy, and the marginalized. He became one of them. He did this to make us rich. He entered the lives of the lowly and raised them up, imbuing their poverty with his own divine dignity. He also endured the worst of deaths to conquer death itself. From first to last, he shared our entire human life so that we could share in the riches of his divine life.

Likewise, Jesus' obedience during the hidden years of his life helped atone for our disobedience. The Gospels don't tell us much about Jesus' life between his birth and his public ministry, but the Gospel of Luke summarizes these years growing up with Mary and Joseph as follows:

> And he went down with them and came to Nazareth, and was obedient to them; and his mother kept all these things in her heart. (Luke 2:51)

It's an amazing concept to wrap our minds around: Jesus, the all-powerful Son of God, was obedient to his human mother and foster father. As such, his obedience and the harmony of the Holy Family are models for our own families and relationships. That obedience also prepared him for the obedience he would give to the Father in offering his life on the Cross.

Jesus' preaching also played a role in our redemption, purifying our consciences with the words he preached, as he says, "You are already made clean by the word which I have spoken to you" (John 15:3).

Jesus' preaching shows us the way to true holiness and purity of heart: following him and loving God and our neighbor as he showed us. It also helps us see that his word has the power to forgive and heal us. He forgave and healed the paralyzed man with his word (Matt 9:1–8), and he forgives and heals us through the sacraments today. In this way, he cleanses our consciences from sin and gives us power to live in holiness.

Jesus also brought redemption by having compassion on those around him, healing them and freeing them from the devil: "He took our infirmities and bore our diseases" (Matt 8:17; Isa 53:4).

The word "compassion" means "suffering with." Jesus took our sufferings upon himself by becoming one of us, enduring the sufferings of human life and the temptations of the devil. He also offered healing and deliverance to those who suffered.

When Jesus comes again in glory, he will take away all suffering and deliver us completely from the power of Satan, but until then we can still call on his compassion now in prayer for comfort, strength, and healing. Moreover, since we are called to love as he loved, we must show his compassion to those around us who are suffering, both by standing by them and by working to relieve their suffering.

Jesus' entire life is a mystery of redemption, but this mystery is most fully realized in his death and Resurrection: he "was put to death for our trespasses and raised for our justification" (Rom 4:25).

By pouring out his life on the Cross, Jesus made his poverty complete. By following the Father's will to the very end, he perfected his obedience. By laying down his life for us, he fulfilled the law of love that he preached to us. By sharing our suffering even to death, he showed ultimate compassion. He gave his life for our sin. He endured the consequences of sin to the end, and in his Resurrection, he conquered sin and its consequences.

Through the mystery of redemption brought to completion in the Cross and Resurrection, we receive justification—we are freed from sin and made holy.

SELECTED READING

Pope St. John Paul II, Encyclical Letter *Redemptor Hominis* (March 4, 1979), nos. 7–8

The Church does not cease to listen to [Christ's] words. She rereads them continually. With the greatest devotion she reconstructs every detail of his life. These words are listened to also by non-Christians. The life of Christ speaks, also, to many who are not capable of repeating with Peter: "You are the Christ, the Son of the living God." He, the Son of the living God, speaks to people also as Man: it is his life that speaks, his humanity, his fidelity to the truth, his all-embracing love. Furthermore, his death on the Cross speaks—that is to say the inscrutable depth of his suffering and abandonment. The Church never ceases to relive his death on the Cross and his Resurrection, which constitute the content of the Church's daily life. Indeed, it is by the command of Christ himself, her Master, that the Church unceasingly celebrates the Eucharist, finding in it the "fountain of life and holiness," the efficacious sign of grace and reconciliation with God, and the pledge of eternal life. The Church lives his mystery, draws unwearyingly from it and continually seeks ways of bringing this mystery of her Master and Lord to humanity—to the peoples, the nations, the succeeding generations, and every individual human being—as if she were ever repeating, as the Apostle did:

"For I decided to know nothing among you except Jesus Christ and him crucified." The Church stays within the sphere of the mystery of the Redemption, which has become the fundamental principle of her life and mission.

The Redeemer of the world! In him has been revealed in a new and more wonderful way the fundamental truth concerning creation to which the Book of Genesis gives witness when it repeats several times: "God saw that it was good." The good has its source in Wisdom and Love. In Jesus Christ the visible world which God created for man—the world that, when sin entered, "was subjected to futility"—recovers again its original link with the divine source of Wisdom and Love. Indeed, "God so loved the world that he gave his only Son." As this link was broken in the man Adam, so in the Man Christ it was reforged. Are we of the twentieth century not convinced of the over poweringly eloquent words of the Apostle of the Gentiles concerning the "creation (that) has been groaning in travail together until now" and "waits with eager longing for the revelation of the sons of God," the creation that "was subjected to futility"? Does not the previously unknown immense progress—which has taken place especially in the course of this century—in the field of man's dominion over the world itself reveal—to a previously unknown degree—that manifold subjection "to futility"? It is enough to recall certain phenomena, such as the threat of pollution of the natural environment in areas of rapid industrialization, or the armed conflicts continually breaking out over and over again, or the prospectives of self-destruction through the use of atomic, hydrogen, neutron and similar weapons, or the lack of respect for the life of the unborn. The world of the new age, the world of space flights, the world of the previously unattained conquests of science and technology—is it not also the world "groaning in travail" that "waits with eager longing for the revealing of the sons of God"?

In its penetrating analysis of "the modern world," the Second Vatican Council reached that most important point of the visible world that is man, by penetrating like Christ the depth of human consciousness and by making contact with the inward mystery of

> man, which in Biblical and non-Biblical language is expressed by the word "heart." Christ, the Redeemer of the world, is the one who penetrated in a unique unrepeatable way into the mystery of man and entered his "heart." Rightly therefore does the Second Vatican Council teach: "The truth is that only in the mystery of the Incarnate Word does the mystery of man take on light. For Adam, the first man, was a type of him who was to come (*Rom* 5:14), Christ the Lord. Christ the new Adam, in the very revelation of the mystery of the Father and of his love, *fully reveals man to himself* and brings to light his most high calling." And the Council continues: "He who is the 'image of the invisible God' (*Col* 1:15), is himself the perfect man who has restored in the children of Adam that likeness to God which had been disfigured ever since the first sin. Human nature, by the very fact that it was assumed, not absorbed, in him, has been raised in us also to a dignity beyond compare. For, by his Incarnation, he, the son of God, *in a certain way united himself with each man*. He worked with human hands, he thought with a human mind. He acted with a human will, and with a human heart he loved. Born of the Virgin Mary, he has truly been made one of us, like to us in all things except sin," he, the Redeemer of man.

QUESTIONS FOR REVIEW

1. How does the angel Gabriel tell Mary she will become pregnant with Jesus?
2. What does the angel Gabriel mean when he calls Mary "full of grace"?
3. Name one prophecy from the Old Testament that Jesus fulfilled.
4. What was the purpose of the Incarnation?
5. What was Jesus' ultimate act of obedience to the Father and act of compassion for us?

QUESTIONS FOR DISCUSSION

1. What is one thing you learned about God the Father's love from Jesus' life on earth? Explain.
2. Our culture is fixated on wealth and material success, but Jesus lived on earth as a poor man. What does this tell us about wealth and poverty?
3. Jesus had great compassion on us. Who is someone you know that has had compassion on you? Describe what happened. What is one way you could have compassion on someone else?

Part III

The Light of Salvation: Redemption Unfolds

At the beginning of every Easter Vigil Mass, the faithful process into a completely darkened church behind the Easter candle, which is carried by the deacon. Entering the church and processing to the altar, the deacon stops three times and proclaims "Lumen Christi," which means "The light of Christ." At the same time, the believers in the church light a taper from the Easter candle, slowly passing "the light of Christ" to their neighbors, who in turn light their own candles from their neighbors' candles. By the time the Easter candle reaches the alter, the Church is bathed in candlelight. Dating back to the earliest days of Christianity, this practice—known as *Lucernarium*—is a powerful representation of Jesus Christ, our light, saving us from the darkness of sin.

In Part III, we will examine Jesus' public ministry more closely, looking at how his saving mission brought light into the world.

Chapter 1

The Beginning of Jesus' Public Ministry

Jesus Is Baptized by John

Jesus' public life and ministry began with his baptism in the Jordan River. At that time, John the Baptist was baptizing crowds of people at the Jordan "for the forgiveness of sins" (Luke 3:3). Some people wondered whether John the Baptist was the Messiah, but John told them that he was not:

> As the people were in expectation, and all men questioned in their hearts concerning John, whether perhaps he were the Christ, John answered them all, "I baptize you with water; but he who is mightier than I is coming, the thong of whose sandals I am not worthy to untie; he will baptize you with the Holy Spirit and with fire." (Luke 3:15–16)

"He who is mightier than I" referred to Jesus, who stood in the crowd of people waiting to be baptized.

John then baptized Jesus, and God the Father and the Holy Spirit revealed him as the Messiah and the Son of God:

> Now when all the people were baptized, and when Jesus also had been baptized and was praying, the heaven was opened, and the Holy Spirit descended upon him in bodily form, as a dove, and a voice came from heaven, "You are my beloved Son; with you I am well pleased." (Luke 3:21–22)

All three Persons of the Holy Trinity were present in this scene: Jesus, the Son of God, was in the river; God the Father opened the heavens and revealed the divine Personhood of Jesus; and the Holy Spirit appeared as a dove, revealing that Jesus is the Messiah or Christ—the one anointed by the Spirit (Isa 61:1).

Why, though, was it necessary for Jesus to be baptized at all? He had no sin. He had no need for forgiveness. The Gospel of Matthew answers that question when it says Jesus was baptized to "fulfil all righteousness" (Matt 3:15). In other words, he underwent baptism as God's Suffering Servant, submitting himself entirely to the Father's will, allowing himself to be numbered among sinners (CCC 535–536).

In that, Jesus showed us the way to attain forgiveness. At his baptism, Jesus went down into the water and rose again, foreshadowing his death, burial, and Resurrection. In turn, through the Sacrament of Baptism, Christians are made like Jesus and participate in his death and Resurrection (Rom 6:4). As St. Hilary of Poitiers (ca. 300–368) states:

> Everything that happened to Christ lets us know that, after the bath of water, the Holy Spirit swoops down upon us from high heaven and that, adopted by the Father's voice, we become the sons of God.[1]

When we enter the waters of Baptism and emerge to be reborn of water and spirit, the Holy Spirit descends on us too, and we become part of the family of Christ—adopted sons and daughters of the Father (CCC 537).

---

1 St. Hilary of Poitiers, *In Matth.* 2, 5: PL 9, 927, cited in CCC 537.

Jesus Is Tempted by the Devil

Assigned Reading
Matthew 4:1–11

After his baptism, Jesus went to the desert to fast and pray for forty days. There, Satan tempted him to reject his Father's will.

First, Satan told Jesus, "If you are the Son of God, command these stones to become loaves of bread" (Matt 4:3). Jesus was presumably hungry after forty days in the desert without food, but more than turning stones into bread, Satan tried to tempt Jesus to turn away from his Father's will and use his power for his own purposes. Jesus rejected that temptation, answering Satan with the words of Sacred Scripture: "Man shall not live by bread alone, but by every word that proceeds from the mouth of God" (Matt 4:4; Deut 8:3). This reference to the Law in the Old Testament signified his complete obedience to the Father.

In the second temptation, Satan took Jesus to the top of the temple in Jerusalem and told him that if he really was the Son of God, he could throw himself off the temple and angels would come to save him (Matt 4:5–6). Jesus, however, refused to use his power to prove his divinity in this way, and again quoting Scripture said, "You shall not tempt the Lord your God" (Matt 4:7; Deut 6:16).

For the third temptation, Satan offered Jesus all the kingdoms of the world if he would bow down and worship him (Matt 4:8–9). Jesus refused this final temptation to gain worldly power and rebuked Satan, saying, "Begone, Satan! for it is written, 'You shall worship the Lord your God and him only shall you serve'" (Matt 4:10; Deut 6:13). After this, Satan left him and angels minister to Jesus.

What Satan tried to do, in all three instances, was tempt Jesus to use his power for himself: to satisfy his desires, to gain wealth and power, and to enjoy the glory and adoration of the world. However, none of these represented the will of God. Jesus had a specific ministry and mission, and he would not allow himself to be swayed from it.

As we learned earlier, Jesus is the "New Adam." Like the first Adam, Jesus was tempted, but unlike him, he didn't sin. He successfully rejected temptation and remained obedient to his Father in all things. The Catechism explains, "The temptation in the desert shows Jesus, the humble Messiah, who triumphs over Satan by his total adherence to the plan of salvation willed by the Father" (CCC 566).

Jesus also had to resist his followers' expectations about what it meant for him to be the Messiah. Several disciples wanted Jesus to be a worldly, powerful Messiah who would make everything right in this world through force. For example, in Matthew 16:21–23, when Jesus began to share the plan of his trial and death in Jerusalem, Peter protested, saying, "God forbid, Lord! This shall never happen to you" (Matt 16:22). Jesus immediately rebuked him, exclaiming, "Get behind me, Satan!" (Matt 16:23).

Through his temptations in the desert, Jesus "[vanquishes] the Tempter for us" (CCC 540). He overcame the power that Satan had over us because of Adam and Eve's disobedience. Since he was fully human, Jesus went through every kind of trial, but he did not sin. As the writer of Hebrews says about Jesus, "For we have not a high priest who is unable to sympathize with our weaknesses, but one who in every respect has been tempted as we are, yet without sinning" (Heb 4:15).

In all this, Jesus shows us that, through the grace of our Baptism we, too, can overcome temptation, growing holier through that very struggle.

The Miracle at Cana

Assigned Reading
John 2:1–11

At a wedding feast in Cana, Jesus changed water into wine. This was the first public "sign," or miracle, that he performed in the Gospels (John 2:11).

Note the contrast between this miracle and the miracles that Satan tempted Jesus to perform. Jesus performed the miracle not for himself but in response to someone else's need, and he didn't make a big show of it to impress the crowd. The steward and the bridegroom didn't even know what had happened, but Mary and his disciples understood and "believed in him" (John 2:11).

This first sign of Jesus' is rich with symbols that are important throughout the Bible. First, it's important that this first sign happens at a wedding feast. Remember, the covenantal union of God with his people Israel and of Christ with his Church are both compared to the union of a man and woman in marriage (see Jer 2:1; Eph 5:22–23), and Scripture repeatedly speaks of the celebration of this union as a wedding feast (see Exod 24:9–11; Mark 2:18–20; Matt 22:1–14; Rev 19:7–9; 21:2). Even more fundamentally, the wedding feast at Cana and Jesus' miracle there prefigure the Eucharist, the thanksgiving meal of the New Covenant, where Jesus miraculously gives us his Flesh and Blood under the appearances of bread and wine (CCC 1335).

Also important here is that Jesus' first miracle was initiated by his mother, Mary. The newly married couple didn't seem to have any idea of the problem, but Mary saw their need and approached her Son. This shows us Mary's sensitivity to the needs of the wedding hosts, who might have been embarrassed if they ran out of wine at the feast. Then, even though he had not started his public ministry yet, Jesus responded to his mother's concern that "They have no wine" (John 2:3). He changed the jars of water into wine; in fact, it's the finest wine at the feast.

Here again, Mary appears as the "New Eve." Where Eve prompted Adam to sin, Mary prompted Jesus to begin his work of redemption. In this role, we see how Mary also prays and intercedes for us with Jesus. We can go to Mary with our needs because she is closer to Jesus than any other human being. She intercedes with him, and he hears her prayer. Finally, she says to us, as she did to the servants at Cana, "Do whatever he tells you" (John 2:5). These are the last recorded words of Mary in the Bible, and they are her directions to us. Mary points us to Jesus and tells us to follow him (CCC 2618).

SELECTED READING

Pope St. John Paul II, Encyclical Letter on the Blessed Virgin Mary in the Life of the Pilgrim Church *Redemptoris Mater* (March 25, 1987), nos. 21–22

Mary is present at Cana in Galilee as the Mother of Jesus, and in a significant way she contributes to that "beginning of the signs" which reveal the messianic power of her Son. We read: "When the wine gave out, the mother of Jesus said to him, 'They have no wine.' And Jesus said to her, 'O woman, what have you to do with me? My hour has not yet come'" (Jn. 2:3–4). In John's Gospel that "hour" means the time appointed by the Father when the Son accomplishes his task and is to be glorified (cf. Jn. 7:30; 8:20; 12:23, 27; 13:1; 17:1; 19:27). Even though Jesus' reply to his mother sounds like a refusal (especially if we consider the blunt statement "My hour has not yet come" rather than the question), Mary nevertheless turns to the servants and says to them: "Do whatever he tells you" (Jn. 2:5). Then Jesus orders the servants to fill the stone jars with water, and the water becomes wine, better than the wine which has previously been served to the wedding guests.

What deep understanding existed between Jesus and his mother? How can we probe the mystery of their intimate spiritual union? But the fact speaks for itself. It is certain that that event already quite clearly outlines the new dimension, the new meaning of Mary's motherhood. Her motherhood has a significance which is not exclusively contained in the words of Jesus and in the various episodes reported by the Synoptics (Lk. 11:27–28 and Lk. 8:19–21; Mt. 12:46–50; Mk. 3:31–35). In these texts Jesus means above all to contrast the motherhood resulting from the fact of birth with what this "motherhood" (and also "brotherhood") is to be in the dimension of the Kingdom of God, in the salvific radius of God's fatherhood. In John's text on the other hand, the description of the Cana event outlines what is actually manifested as a new kind of motherhood according to the spirit and not just according to the flesh, that is to say Mary's solicitude for human beings, her coming to them in the wide variety of their wants and needs. At Cana in Galilee there is shown only one concrete aspect of human need, apparently a small one of little importance ("They have no wine"). But it has a symbolic value: this coming to the aid of human needs means, at the same time, bringing those needs within the radius of Christ's messianic mission and salvific power. Thus there is a mediation: Mary places herself between her Son and mankind in the reality of their wants, needs and sufferings. She puts herself "in the middle," that is to say she acts as a mediatrix not as an outsider, but in her position as mother. She knows that as such she can point out to her Son the needs of mankind, and in fact, she "has the right" to do so. Her mediation is thus in the nature of intercession: Mary "intercedes" for mankind. And that is not all. As a mother she also wishes the messianic power of her Son to be manifested, that salvific power of his which is meant to help man in his misfortunes, to free him from the evil which in various forms and degrees weighs heavily upon his life. Precisely as the Prophet Isaiah had foretold about the Messiah in the famous passage which Jesus quoted before his fellow townsfolk in Nazareth: "To preach good news to the poor . . . to proclaim release to the captives and recovering of sight to the blind . . ." (cf. Lk. 4:18).

Another essential element of Mary's maternal task is found in her words to the servants: "Do whatever he tells you." The Mother of Christ presents herself as the spokeswoman of her Son's will, pointing out those things which must be done so that the salvific power of the Messiah may be manifested. At Cana, thanks to the intercession of Mary and the obedience of the servants, Jesus begins "his hour." At Cana Mary appears as believing in Jesus. Her faith evokes his first "sign" and helps to kindle the faith of the disciples.

We can therefore say that in this passage of John's Gospel we find as it were a first manifestation of the truth concerning Mary's maternal care. This truth has also found expression in the teaching of the Second Vatican Council. It is important to note how the Council illustrates Mary's maternal role as it relates to the mediation of Christ. Thus we read: "Mary's maternal function towards mankind in no way obscures or diminishes the unique mediation of Christ, but rather shows its efficacy," because "there is one mediator between God and men, the man Christ Jesus" (1 Tim. 2:5). This maternal role of Mary flows, according to God's good pleasure, "from the superabundance of the merits of Christ; it is founded on his mediation, absolutely depends on it, and draws all its efficacy from it." It is precisely in this sense that the episode at Cana in Galilee offers us a sort of first announcement of Mary's mediation, wholly oriented towards Christ and tending to the revelation of his salvific power.

QUESTIONS FOR REVIEW

1. In what way was each member of the Holy Trinity present at Jesus' baptism?
2. Why was it necessary for Jesus to be baptized, even though he was without sin?
3. What, ultimately, did Satan attempt Jesus to do?
4. How did Jesus combat these temptations?
5. What was the first public miracle Jesus performed?

QUESTIONS FOR DISCUSSION

1. What are three temptations you face regularly?
2. Has anything helped you overcome these temptations? If so, what? If not, what can you learn from the way Jesus handled temptation?
3. At Cana, Mary interceded for the bride and groom in their hour of need. Do you ever ask Mary to intercede for you? Why or why not?

Chapter 2

The Height of Jesus' Active Ministry

Jesus Announces the Kingdom of God

After John the Baptist was arrested by Herod, Jesus began to travel and preach in Galilee, saying, "The time is fulfilled, and the kingdom of God is at hand; repent, and believe in the gospel" (Mark 1:15).

The kingdom was the primary theme of Jesus' earthly ministry. It was, more than anything else, what he preached about as he traveled throughout Judea. This is because the Father's will is to raise us up to share in his divine life, and he does this by gathering us around his Son, Jesus, the Son of David, in the Church, which is the beginning of the kingdom of God on earth (CCC 541). Jesus calls people into this gathering by preaching, miracles, and sending out his disciples, and he accomplishes the coming of his kingdom through his Paschal Mystery—his death and Resurrection. He says, "I, when I am lifted up from the earth [on the Cross], will draw all men to myself" (John 12:32; CCC 542).

While the kingdom of God is a mystery that won't be fully realized on earth until Jesus comes in glory, we can learn a few important things about it from the preaching of Jesus:

1. Everyone is called to enter the kingdom. Jesus preached to the people around him in his hometown and throughout his region, but the Good News of Jesus is intended to reach everyone in the whole world: "First announced to the children of Israel, this messianic kingdom is intended to accept men of all nations [Cf. *Mt* 8:11 10:5–7; 28:19]" (CCC 543).
2. "The kingdom belongs to the *poor and lowly,* which means those who have accepted it with humble hearts" (CCC 544). Jesus comes to the lowly people of the world, and he "shares the life of the poor, from the cradle to the cross; he experiences hunger, thirst, and privation [Cf. *Mt* 21:18; *Mk* 2:23–26; *Jn* 4:6–7; 19:28; *Lk* 9:58]" (CCC 544). He also chose ordinary people, such as fishermen and tax collectors, to be his disciples. The Father revealed to them what was hidden from the wise and learned.
3. Jesus reaches out to sinners and invites them to the kingdom, saying, "I came not to call the righteous, but sinners" (Mark 2:17). Jesus calls sinners to conversion, which is necessary for entering the kingdom, but he emphasizes the extravagant mercy of God in forgiving sin and the joy over one who repents (see the Parable of the Lost Sheep, Luke 15:3–7; and the Parable of the Prodigal Son, Luke 15:11–32). Above all he proves God's mercy by giving up his own life on the Cross for our sins (CCC 545).
4. Jesus also made it clear that the coming of the kingdom will bring judgment. Several parables tell of the accounting each individual must give of their time on earth, that everything secret will be made known. Each individual will be judged at the moment of death according to his or her actions at the Particular Judgment, and Christ will make all things known and judge all creation at the General Judgment at the end of time (see the Parable of the Talents, Matt 25:14–30; and Matt 25:31–46).

Jesus Proclaims the Kingdom through Parables

Jesus frequently proclaimed the kingdom of God through parables—simple images or comparisons that reveal some aspect of the kingdom. Jesus' parables are deceptively simple because they are short and use everyday images, but to those who hear them with faith, they teach profound truths about the kingdom.

Let's examine a few of them along with Jesus' explanation of his teaching in Matthew 13.

> **Assigned Reading**
> Matthew 13:1–50

Some of Jesus' parables explain how the kingdom will grow and be revealed. He compared the kingdom of heaven to a mustard seed, which is the smallest of seeds, but grows into the largest of shrubs (Matt 13:31–32). Just so, the kingdom starts on earth with Jesus and his small group of disciples, but grows into the Church, which will gather in people from all nations. The meaning of the parable of the leaven (Matt 13:33) is similar: a nearly invisible amount of yeast makes an enormous amount of flour rise, like the small number of Christ's followers work, often in hidden ways, until the whole world is transformed.

Other parables explain how the judgment between good and evil will occur. Jesus told the parable of the weeds among the wheat (Matt 13:24–30) and then later explained it privately to his disciples, telling them that the devil is still at work in this age, tempting us to sin, and so good and evil coexist in the Church. But God is patient, not wanting to destroy the good along with the wicked. He withholds his judgment until the end of the age, when all things will be made clear. The parable of the net is similar: judgment will occur, but God is patient, waiting until the net is full.

Then, there are parables that deal with our response to the preaching of the kingdom. They "confront the hearer or reader with a radical choice about his invitation to enter the Kingdom of God" (CCC Glossary). The parables of the hidden treasure and the pearl of great price illustrate the radical choice demanded by the preaching of the kingdom. A man finds a treasure or a valuable pearl and immediately goes and sells everything he owns to acquire it (Matt 13:44–46). This tells us that the kingdom is so valuable that we should be ready to give up everything we have to enter it: "For what will it profit a man, if he gains the whole world and forfeits his life?" (Matt 16:26).

The parable of the sower explains how different people respond to the invitation to enter the kingdom (Matt 13:1–9, 18–23). Some reject it outright. Others respond with joy, but then give up when the way proves too hard. Others allow the worries of everyday life to overshadow the importance of the kingdom. And some give their whole life to attain it.

Hearing and doing the word of Jesus is required of his followers in order to enter the kingdom, but those who do so will bring forth fruit, an amazing abundance, "a hundredfold" (Matt 13:8). The Catechism explains that "the parables are like mirrors for man: will he be hard soil or good earth for the word [Cf. *Mt* 13:3–9]?" Deeds are required, not just words (CCC 546).

The Signs of the Kingdom

> **Assigned Reading**
> Matthew 9:2–8

Just as Jesus' parables help us understand the kingdom, Jesus' many miracles bear witness to the truth that he is the Messiah and that the kingdom is present in him. As Jesus said, "the works which the Father has granted me to accomplish, these very works which I am doing, bear me witness that the Father has sent me" (John 5:36). Accordingly, when the disciples of John the Baptist came to ask if Jesus was the Messiah, Jesus pointed right back to the signs he worked, which were foretold by the prophet Isaiah (Isa 35:5–6; 61:1):

> Go and tell John what you have seen and heard: the blind receive their sight, the lame walk, lepers are cleansed, and the deaf hear,

> the dead are raised up, the poor have good news preached to them. And blessed is he who takes no offense at me. (Luke 7:22–23)

Jesus' miracles testify to his power to heal all types of illness and distress. He reached out to cure people possessed by demons, who were excluded from society, and he even brought people back from the dead, demonstrating his power over creation. Here are some examples of different types of miracles worked by Jesus:

Exorcisms: Mark 1:23–28; 5:1–20; Luke 4:33–37
Healings: Mark 2:1–12; 3:1–6; Luke 17:11–19; John 5:1–9; 9:1–41
Resurrections: Luke 7:11–17; 8:40–56; John 11:1–45
Control over nature: Matthew 8:23–27; Luke 5:1–11; John 6:16–21

Jesus attracted a great crowd of people by his teaching and his miracles, but as at Cana, he didn't perform miracles just to show off his power or satisfy the crowd's curiosity or desire for magic. Then and now, his miracles are evidence that he comes from the Father. They invite people to believe in him, and they strengthen the faith of those who already believe. But, like his teaching in parables, the significance of the signs of the kingdom is lost on those who "take offense" at him. Many saw the signs and still rejected him. Some even accused him of performing miracles by the power of the devil (Mark 3:22; CCC 548).

This is true today as well. Some people dismiss Jesus' miracles as impossibilities or myths made up by later writers, but the accounts of miracles are part of the earliest accounts of Jesus:

> Even the oldest sources tell of numerous miracles, even the raising of the dead, as a confirmation of Jesus' preaching: "But if it is by the Spirit of God that I cast out demons, then the Kingdom of God has come upon you" (Mt. 12:28). The miracles took place in public; some of the persons involved were

> known by name, for instance, blind Bartimaeus (Mk. 10:46–52) or Peter's mother-in-law (Mt. 8:14–15). There were also miracles that in those Jewish circles were considered shocking and outrageous (for example, the cure of a crippled man on the Sabbath, the cure of lepers). Nevertheless they were not disputed by contemporary Judaism.[1]

The miracle accounts in the Gospels also witness to the reaction of the people who followed Jesus. They saw him change impossible situations—healing the sick and raising the dead—and because of that believed that he was the Messiah, the Son of God (see Matt 8:27; 12:23; Mark 7:37; Luke 9:43).

In the short story of the healing of a paralyzed man, assigned above, we see several things that we have already discussed. First, we see the role of faith. Jesus offered healing and forgiveness in response to the faith of the paralyzed man and his friends. The miracle demonstrates the authority that Jesus has been given by the Father, but the scribes lacked faith and took offense at him, while those who believed glorified God for giving authority to forgive and heal to men.

Notice, however, that Jesus' first response to their faith was to offer the man forgiveness for his sins and that he healed the paralyzed man to demonstrate that he has the authority to forgive sins. During his life on earth, Jesus miraculously delivered some people from evils, like hunger, illness, and even death, all to demonstrate that he has authority—that he is the Messiah, the Son of God, and that the kingdom has arrived in him. However, his mission wasn't to take away all earthly evils, but to free us from slavery to sin (CCC 549).

The kingdom of God means the defeat of the kingdom of Satan and his reign over us. Jesus cast out demons to demonstrate his authority over Satan, and through his life, death, and Resurrection he broke the dominion that Satan had gained over humanity through sin (CCC 550).

---

[1] Cardinal Christoph Schönborn, ed., *Youcat English: Youth Catechism of the Catholic Church*, trans. Michael J. Miller (San Francisco: Ignatius Press, 2011), Q. 90.

The Keys of the Kingdom

Jesus established his Church on earth to be "the seed and the beginning of the kingdom" (CCC 541), and he chose twelve men, the Apostles, to be the foundation of his Church (Rev 21:14). The number twelve is significant because it signifies that the Church is the restoration of the kingdom of Israel, which was made up of the twelve tribes. The Apostles shared in Jesus' ministry from the beginning, and he gave them a share in his authority, sending them out to preach and heal.

Among the Twelve, Jesus gave a specific authority and mission to Peter. After Peter professed that Jesus is the Christ, the Son of the living God, Jesus told him, "you are Peter, and on this rock I will build my Church, and the gates of Hades shall not prevail against it" (Matt 16:18). In response to Peter's profession of faith, Jesus made him the rock of the Church, with a particular mission to protect this faith and strengthen the other Apostles (Luke 22:32; CCC 552).

Jesus then continued, saying to Peter, "I will give you the keys of the kingdom of heaven, and whatever you bind on earth shall be bound in heaven, and whatever you loose on earth shall be loosed in heaven" (Matt 16:19). By this, Jesus meant he was giving Peter the authority to govern the Church. The power to bind and loose is the authority "to absolve sins, to pronounce doctrinal judgments, and to make disciplinary decisions in the Church" (CCC 553). The other Apostles also received the power to bind and loose (Matt 18:18), but only Peter received the keys of the kingdom, signifying his particular role as head of the Apostles.

Today, the ministry and authority entrusted to the Apostles continues to be exercised by the bishops of the Church, who are their successors, and the special role of Peter is exercised by the pope, who is the successor of Peter in particular.

The Transfiguration

After Peter's confession that Jesus is the Son of God, Jesus began to tell them about how he had to go to Jerusalem to suffer, die, and be raised again. Despite the fact that he had just professed faith in Jesus, Peter couldn't understand this prediction, and he rebuked Jesus, forbidding that it should happen (Matt 16:21–23).

Several days later, Jesus took Peter, James, and John up a mountain with him and was transfigured before them. Jesus' face and clothing became "dazzling white" (Luke 9:29), and he conversed with the prophet Elijah and Moses, who also appeared, discussing what must happen in Jerusalem. Peter, James, and John witnessed all this. They also witnessed the cloud that suddenly overshadowed them and, as at Jesus' baptism, heard a voice from heaven say, "This is my Son, my Chosen; listen to him!" (Luke 9:35). After this, Moses and Elijah disappeared.

The Transfiguration gave Peter, James, and John a glimpse of Jesus' divine glory. It also confirmed Peter's confession, as well Jesus' prediction of his Passion. Its purpose was to strengthen the faith of the Apostles to prepare them for Jesus' Passion (CCC 568).

Moses and Elijah's presence is also important. Together, they represent the Law and the prophets. In the Old Testament, both Moses and Elijah had encountered God on the mountain (Exod 24:18; 1 Kgs 19:8–18). As at Jesus' Transfiguration, God showed his presence to Moses in a cloud, and Moses' encounter with God caused his face to shine so that others couldn't look at it (Exod 34:29). Jesus, Moses, and Elijah discussed Jesus' "departure" and what he was going to accomplish in Jerusalem—that is, the Paschal Mystery of his suffering, death, and Resurrection, which he had just foretold to his disciples. Through his Paschal Mystery, he would fulfill the Law and the Prophets as God's Suffering Servant (CCC 555).

The Transfiguration also parallels Jesus' baptism in several ways. At Jesus' baptism, his divinity was revealed in preparation for the beginning of his ministry by a voice from the heavens and the Holy Spirit descending on him. At his Transfiguration, his divinity was revealed again in preparation for his suffering, death, and Resurrection by the voice and the cloud, which indicates the presence of the Holy Spirit. As at his baptism, all three Persons of the Holy Trinity were present. But, while Jesus' baptism points to our Baptism, through which we are first reborn, his Transfiguration points to our resurrection at the end of time, when we will rise again and be glorified like he was (CCC 555–556).

SELECTED READING

Scott Hahn, "The Third Luminous Mystery: The Proclamation of the Kingdom," in *Catholic for a Reason II: Scripture and the Mystery of the Mother of God*, pp. 159–161

Jesus promised a kingdom, and it was a kingdom His countrymen had long awaited. He told them that the kingdom was "at hand" and "near" (Mt. 3:2, 4:17, 10:7; Lk. 21:31).

For many would-be believers, the scandal of Christianity is this apparently unfulfilled promise. Jesus said the kingdom of God was coming soon. Yet, two thousand years later, people are still scanning the skies and the calendars for signs of His reign. As the apostate scholar Alfred Loisy put it: Jesus came promising the kingdom, but all He left us was the Church.

Here's news: The kingdom has already come. It's here, and it's going to stay forever.

Many people today misunderstand the "kingdom of God" as the "reign" or "cosmic government" of God—apart from any earthly manifestation of a monarchical realm. But, for the first-century Jews, "the kingdom" was no such abstract concept. God had always ruled the earth as its Creator and Lord, and He would always do so. "The kingdom" meant something else, something very specific. It was the divinely promised and long-awaited restoration of the royal House of David.

God Himself had promised this: the Son of David would be the Son of God, and He would reign forever: "I will raise up your offspring after you, who shall come forth from your body. . . . *I will be his father, and he shall be my son*" (2 Sam. 7:12–14; see also 1 Chron. 17:13, 1 Chron. 28:6). The divine sonship of the Son of David was celebrated in the Jerusalem liturgy: "He shall cry to me, 'Thou art my Father.' . . . I will make him the first-born, the highest of the kings of the earth" (Ps. 89:26–27).

God had made an everlasting covenant with David and his descendants. The Son of David would rule—as the Son of God—over Israel and the nations *forever.*

David's dynasty did indeed last a long time—five hundred years—but that's hardly forever. Since God had made a promise, His people expected Him to make good on it.

The apostles, like Catholics today, dared to take Jesus at His word and accepted His promise on His terms. He promised us a glorious kingdom within His own generation—and we boldly proclaim that He made good on that promise. For all time, Jesus has established His Eucharistic Kingdom, the Church.

The Church is God's kingdom, here and now. We must admit, however, that it doesn't always appear so glorious. But Jesus never said it would be paradise. His kingdom-parables speak instead of wheat growing alongside weeds, of dragnets taking in both holy mackerel and unholy muck.

So our Lord promised us a kingdom, and He left us the Church. Yet there is no contradiction, no unfulfilled promise. What Jesus promised and what He delivered are one and the same. He said the kingdom is near—and it is. It's as near as your local parish.

The kingdom is where the king is present. Where the Eucharist is, there is the King. The kingdom is already on earth, because the Church, the Eucharistic Kingdom, is already in heaven.

Lord Jesus, in every Mass I pray to the Father, "Thy kingdom come!" Help my unbelief. Help me to believe that my prayer has been answered—in spite of the scandals of the day and the weakness of my own will. May I love Your Church with all my heart. May I proclaim Your kingdom, come among us even now, with the witness of my life and my words.

QUESTIONS FOR REVIEW

1. Who is called to enter the kingdom of God?
2. What form does the kingdom of God take on earth?
3. What is a parable? Give one example of a parable used by Jesus in the Gospels.
4. What was the ultimate purpose of Jesus' miracles?
5. To whom did Jesus give the authority to govern his kingdom on earth? Who possesses that authority today?

QUESTIONS FOR DISCUSSION

1. Why do you think the people of Jesus' day had a hard time recognizing him as the Messiah? What would you have expected the Messiah to be like? How was the reality different from those expectations?
2. Do you believe in miracles? Why or why not?
3. How can you proclaim the kingdom of God in your home, school, and community?

Chapter 3

Jesus Institutes the Eucharist

The Last Supper

Assigned Reading
Luke 22:14–23

The Jewish Passover ritual is an annual ceremonial remembrance of when God brought the Israelites out of Egypt. During Passover, unleavened bread and bitter herbs are eaten during a ceremony with special prayers and readings from Scripture to commemorate God's deliverance of the Israelites from slavery and death. By celebrating the Passover with his disciples, Jesus faithfully partook of the ceremony as a Jew, but he also deepened and expanded its meaning. During the Passover with his disciples in Jerusalem, Jesus instituted the Eucharist "as the memorial of his death and Resurrection, and commanded his apostles to celebrate it until his return" (CCC 1337).

> And he took bread, and when he had given thanks he broke it and gave it to them, saying, "This is my body which is given for you. Do this in remembrance of me." And likewise the chalice after supper, saying, "This chalice which is poured out for you is the new covenant in my blood." (Luke 22:19–20)

On the following day, Good Friday, Jesus would give up his body and pour out his blood on the Cross, and the New Covenant would be sealed. This is the Paschal Mystery, which fulfills what the Passover prefigures: Jesus passes over to the Father in his death and Resurrection and delivers us from death and the slavery of sin. But the night before this, he made this mystery present in the Passover meal with his disciples. He took bread and wine, the symbols of the Passover of the Old Covenant, gave thanks, and transformed them into the very Body and Blood he would offer on the Cross in the Passover of the New Covenant (CCC 1340).

This is the Sacrament of the Eucharist, which Jesus commanded his Apostles to continue, saying, "Do this in remembrance of me." This command means something much more than just remembering Jesus' actions. By this command, Jesus instituted his Apostles as priests of the New Covenant. Through them and their successors, the Eucharist is celebrated as "the *memorial* of Christ, of his life, of his death, of his Resurrection, and of his intercession in the presence of the Father [Cf. *2 Cor* 11:26]" (CCC 1341). As at the Last Supper, the Eucharist makes Jesus' Paschal Mystery present. At Mass, bread and wine are truly transformed into his Body and Blood, which were offered on the Cross and raised from the dead. By partaking of Christ's Body and Blood in the Eucharist, we participate in the New Covenant he established in them. Through the Eucharist, Christ and his Paschal Mystery remain present in the Church:

> In order never to depart from his own and to make them sharers in his Passover, he instituted the Eucharist as the memorial of his death and Resurrection, and commanded his apostles to celebrate it until his return. (CCC 1337)

The Real Presence

It's important to understand that the Church doesn't believe the bread and wine consecrated at Mass are just symbols of Jesus' Body and Blood. Rather, the Church holds that the consecrated bread and wine of the Eucharist are the true Body and Blood of Jesus. In them, Jesus is really, truly, and substantially present. This is called the doctrine of the Real Presence.

We find the Scriptural basis for this teaching in John 6:22–58, which is known as the "Bread of Life Discourse." In this passage, Jesus told the crowd, "I am the living bread which came down from heaven; if any one eats of this bread, he will live for ever; and the bread which I shall give for the life of the world is my flesh" (John 6:51). This message was not well received. The people objected, saying, "How can this man give us his flesh to eat?" (John 6:52). But Jesus persisted:

> So Jesus said to them, "Truly, truly, I say to you, unless you eat the flesh of the Son of man and drink his blood, you have no life in you; he who eats my flesh and drinks my blood has eternal life, and I will raise him up at the last day. For my flesh is food indeed, and my blood is drink indeed. He who eats my flesh and drinks my blood abides in me, and I in him. As the living Father sent me, and I live because of the Father, so he who eats me will live because of me. This is the bread which came down from heaven, not such as the fathers ate and died; he who eats this bread will live for ever." (John 6:53–58)

There is no possibility here that Jesus might have just been speaking symbolically or metaphorically. This is made clear when we contrast Jesus' response here to his dialogue with Nicodemus in John 3:3–7. When Nicodemus objected to Jesus' saying that one must be "born again," Jesus clarified what he meant—he distinguished between the symbolic and literal meaning. In John 6, however, Jesus didn't redefine or explain the concept of eating his Body and drinking his Blood in different terms as he did when he told Nicodemus one must be "born of water and Spirit." Rather Jesus *intensified* his language and made it stronger, insisting several times, "Truly, truly, I say to you."

Jesus was insistent about the fact that his Body and Blood are food and drink—so insistent, in fact, that this caused many of Jesus' disciples to turn away from following him, saying, "This is a hard saying; who can listen to it?" (John 6:60). After this, Jesus poses a question to his Apostles:

> Jesus said to the Twelve, "Will you also go away?" Simon Peter answered him, "Lord, to whom shall we go? You have the words of eternal life; and we have believed, and have come to know, that you are the Holy One of God." (John 6:67–69)

The difficult concepts that Jesus expressed in John 6—that he is the bread of life, and that we must eat his Flesh and drink his Blood—are ultimately incomprehensible except by faith. Indeed, the Catechism connects this difficulty back to the Paschal Mystery and the Cross: "The Eucharist and the Cross are stumbling blocks. It is the same mystery and it never ceases to be an occasion of division" (CCC 1336). And yet, we are also called to belief as the Apostles were.

The Eucharist in the Church

From the beginning, the Church has fulfilled the command of Jesus at the Last Supper to carry on the Eucharist as the memorial of his Paschal Mystery, and the Acts of the Apostles depicts how the early Church was centered on the celebration of the "breaking of the bread":

> And they held steadfastly to the apostles' teaching and fellowship, to the breaking of the bread and to the prayers. . . . And day by day, attending the temple together and breaking bread in their homes, they partook of food with glad and generous hearts. (Acts 2:42, 46)

Just as the disciples on the way to Emmaus recognized Jesus in the breaking of the bread (Luke 24:35), the early Church knew Jesus and experienced his presence in the community through the celebration of the Eucharist. The Eucharist is one of many ways in which he fulfills his promise that "I am with you always, to the close of the age" (Matt 28:20).

The Eucharistic liturgy developed quickly into the form that we recognize today. In a report from St. Justin Martyr from about AD 155, we can see what the early liturgy was like.

> On the day we call the day of the sun, all who dwell in the city or country gather in the same place. The memoirs of the apostles and the writings of the prophets are read, as much as time permits. When the reader has finished, he who presides over those gathered admonishes and challenges them to imitate these beautiful things. Then we all rise together and offer prayers for ourselves . . . and for all others, wherever they may be, so that we may be found righteous by our life and actions, and faithful to the commandments, so as to obtain eternal salvation. When the prayers are concluded we exchange the kiss. Then someone brings bread and a cup of water and wine mixed together to him who presides over the brethren. He takes them and offers praise and glory to the Father of the universe, through the name of the Son and of the Holy Spirit and for a considerable time he gives thanks (in Greek: *eucharistian*) that we have been judged worthy of these gifts. When he has concluded the prayers and thanksgivings, all present give voice to an acclamation by saying: "Amen." When he who presides has given thanks and the people have responded, those whom we call deacons give to those present the "eucharisted" bread, wine and water and take them to those who are absent.[1]

In St. Justin's account, which was written almost two thousand years ago, we see the same basic elements that are present in the Mass today:

- readings from the Old and New Testaments;
- a homily on the readings;
- intercessory prayers;
- the exchange of the sign of peace;
- the consecration the bread and wine in a prayer of thanksgiving (Eucharistic Prayer);
- distribution of the consecrated bread and wine; and
- sending the consecrated bread to believers who aren't at the liturgy.

---

[1] Justin Martyr, *1 Apol* 65–67, quoted in CCC 1345.

This tells us there has been a continuity of worship, from Sunday to Sunday, since the first Christians met to break bread down to today (CCC 1343).

Throughout Part III we have considered the way that redemption unfolded through the life of Jesus from his baptism by John to the Last Supper on the night before he died. These major events of the public ministry of Jesus reveal him as the savior of the world and redeemer of men. To those who followed him, they revealed his divinity and his mission in preparation for his death and Resurrection. Today they make up the five Luminous Mysteries (Mysteries of Light) of the Rosary. Having meditated on them, we are now prepared to explore the central events of the Paschal Mystery in the next chapter.

SELECTED READING

Second Vatican Council, Constitution on the Sacred Liturgy *Sacrosanctum Concilium* (December 4, 1963), nos. 6–10

Just as Christ was sent by the Father, so also He sent the apostles, filled with the Holy Spirit. This He did that, by preaching the gospel to every creature, they might proclaim that the Son of God, by His death and resurrection, had freed us from the power of Satan and from death, and brought us into the kingdom of His Father. His purpose also was that they might accomplish the work of salvation which they had proclaimed, by means of sacrifice and sacraments, around which the entire liturgical life revolves. Thus by baptism men are plunged into the paschal mystery of Christ: they die with Him, are buried with Him, and rise with Him; they receive the spirit of adoption as sons "in which we cry: Abba, Father" (Rom. 8:15), and thus become true adorers whom the Father seeks. In like manner, as often as they eat the supper of the Lord they proclaim the death of the Lord until He comes. For that reason, on the very day of Pentecost, when the Church appeared before the world, "those who received the word" of Peter "were baptized." And "they continued steadfastly in the teaching of the apostles and in the communion of the breaking of bread and in prayers . . . praising God and being in favor with all the people" (Acts 2:41–47). From that time onwards the Church has never failed to come together to celebrate the paschal mystery: reading those things "which were in all the scriptures concerning him" (Luke 24:27), celebrating the Eucharist in which "the victory and triumph of his death are again made present," and at the same time giving thanks "to God for his unspeakable gift" (2 Cor. 9:15) in Christ Jesus, "in praise of his glory" (Eph. 1:12), through the power of the Holy Spirit.

To accomplish so great a work, Christ is always present in His Church, especially in her liturgical celebrations. He is present in the sacrifice of the Mass, not only in the person of His minister, "the same now offering, through the ministry of priests, who formerly offered himself on the cross," but especially under the Eucharistic species. By His power He is present in the sacraments, so that when a man baptizes it is really Christ Himself who baptizes. He is present in His word, since it is He Himself who speaks when the holy scriptures are read in the Church. He is present, lastly, when the Church prays and sings, for He promised: "Where two or three are gathered together in my name, there am I in the midst of them" (Matt. 18:20).

Christ indeed always associates the Church with Himself in this great work wherein God is perfectly glorified and men are sanctified. The Church is His beloved Bride who calls to her Lord, and through Him offers worship to the Eternal Father.

Rightly, then, the liturgy is considered as an exercise of the priestly office of Jesus Christ. In the liturgy the sanctification of the man is signified by signs perceptible to the senses, and is effected in a way which corresponds with each of these signs; in the liturgy the whole public worship is performed by the Mystical Body of Jesus Christ, that is, by the Head and His members.

From this it follows that every liturgical celebration, because it is an action of Christ the priest and of His Body which is the Church, is a sacred action surpassing all others; no other action of the Church can equal its efficacy by the same title and to the same degree.

In the earthly liturgy we take part in a foretaste of that heavenly liturgy which is celebrated in the holy city of Jerusalem toward which we journey as pilgrims, where Christ is sitting at the right hand of God, a minister of the holies and of the true tabernacle; we sing a hymn to the Lord's glory with all the warriors of the heavenly army; venerating the memory of the saints, we hope for some part and fellowship with them; we eagerly await the Saviour, Our Lord Jesus Christ, until He, our life, shall appear and we too will appear with Him in glory.

The sacred liturgy does not exhaust the entire activity of the Church. Before men can come to the liturgy they must be called to faith and to conversion: "How then are they to call upon him in whom they have not yet believed? But how are they to believe him whom they have not heard? And how are they to hear if no one preaches? And how are men to preach unless they be sent?" (Rom. 10:14–15).

. . . Nevertheless the liturgy is the summit toward which the activity of the Church is directed; at the same time it is the font from which all her power flows. For the aim and object of apostolic works is that all who are made sons of God by faith and baptism should come together to praise God in the midst of His Church, to take part in the sacrifice, and to eat the Lord's supper.

The liturgy in its turn moves the faithful, filled with "the paschal sacraments," to be "one in holiness"; it prays that "they may hold fast in their lives to what they have grasped by their faith"; the renewal in the Eucharist of the covenant between the Lord and man draws the faithful into the compelling love of Christ and sets them on fire. From the liturgy, therefore, and especially from the Eucharist, as from a font, grace is poured forth upon us; and the sanctification of men in Christ and the glorification of God, to which all other activities of the Church are directed as toward their end, is achieved in the most efficacious possible way.

QUESTIONS FOR REVIEW

1. What does the Passover supper recall?
2. In what ways did the Passover foreshadow the Eucharist?
3. What is the doctrine of the Real Presence?
4. How do we know, based on Scripture, that Jesus wasn't speaking metaphorically when he said we must eat his flesh and drink his blood?
5. What elements of our own liturgy were present in the first days of the Church?

QUESTIONS FOR DISCUSSION

1. Why do you think it is important to receive the Eucharist at least every Sunday, and daily if possible?
2. How could simply spending time with the Eucharist, in prayer, help you grow closer to God?
3. What can make it difficult to believe that Jesus is really present in the Eucharist? Has anything made it easier for you to believe that he is really present?

Part IV

Christ Redeems Us through His Paschal Mystery

In Part III, we studied the major events of Jesus' public ministry, which revealed his divinity and mission of redemption. We now turn to the climactic events of his life—his suffering, death, Resurrection, and Ascension. These are the central events of his Paschal Mystery, which accomplished his mission of redemption.

Chapter 1

The Passion and Death of Jesus

The story of Jesus' Passion is familiar to us because we hear it at Mass every Holy Week, but let's examine it in light of his mission of redemption.

The Agony in the Garden

> **Assigned Reading**
> Mark 14:32–42

After celebrating the Last Supper with his disciples, Jesus went out with them to the garden of Gethsemane to pray. There, he was greatly troubled and pleaded, "Abba, Father, all things are possible to you; remove this chalice from me; yet not what I will, but what you will" (Mark 14:36).

Jesus is fully human, and at Gethsemane, he shared in the horror of death that we experience. Remember that we were made to live forever with God, but death resulted from sin (see Part I, Chapter 2). Consequently, even though we all must die, it troubles us—even terrifies us—because we were meant for eternal life.

At the beginning of his ministry, Jesus overcame the temptation of Satan to turn from the Father's will. Later, he rebuked Peter for trying to divert him from the Cross. At Gethsemane, though, he faced the full weight of human suffering, sin, and death, and the hour of "the power of darkness" (Luke 22:53). On this last night, he felt "greatly distressed and troubled," and said, "My soul is very sorrowful, even to death" (Mark 14:33, 34). He even prayed that, if it were possible, he might be delivered from his Cross. Nevertheless, he accepted the Father's will: "Not what I will, but what you will" (Mark 14:36). And in that, he made his suffering and death redemptive.

The Arrest and Trial of Jesus

Assigned Reading
Mark 14:43–15:15

While Jesus was still in the Garden of Gethsemane, Judas, one of the Twelve Apostles, arrived. With him were soldiers who had come to arrest Jesus. Judas led them there, betraying Jesus for thirty pieces of silver. At first, Peter attempted to stop the soldiers (see John 18:10), but Jesus, submissive to the will of the Father, let himself be taken. All his disciples fled.

The soldiers then led Jesus to the house of the high priest, where he was put on trial before the high priest and the whole council. False witnesses came forward and accused him of saying that he was going to destroy the temple and replace it with one not made by human hands. The high priest asked Jesus to answer to the accusations, but he remained silent. Finally, the high priest asked him directly, "Are you the Christ, the Son of the Blessed?" (Mark 14:61). Jesus, in turn, answered directly, "I am; and you will see the Son of man seated at the right hand of Power, and coming with the clouds of heaven" (Mark 14:62).

Note that "the Blessed" and "the Power" are both terms that Jews used to indicate God, whose name they avoided pronouncing out of reverence. So, what Jesus tells the high priest here is that he is the Son of God. The chief priests, however, not believing Jesus, accused him of blasphemy and condemned him to death in accordance with the Law (Lev 24:16).

Jesus before Pilate

At the time of Jesus, Judea was ruled by the Romans, so the Jewish leaders didn't have the authority to execute Jesus themselves. They had to bring him to the Roman governor, Pontius Pilate. According to other historical sources, Pilate was a cruel governor who violently suppressed several uprisings. So, while the chief priests were concerned about the threat Jesus posed to their religious authority, Pilate was concerned about the threat Jesus posed to the political authority of the Roman Empire. Accordingly, he asked Jesus, "Are you the King of the Jews?" (Mark 15:2).

Jesus had responded clearly to the high priest's question, but his answer to Pilate was less direct: "You have said so" (Mark 15:2).

Jesus came as the Messiah, the Son of King David. Many Jews (even some of Jesus' own disciples), however, expected the Messiah to be a political figure who would deliver them from foreign domination. This was why Herod had tried to destroy Jesus in his infancy (Matt 2). This was also why Pilate was concerned. Jesus, however, wasn't after political power. He is a king, so he didn't deny that before Pilate, but as he explained to Pilate in the Gospel of John, "My kingship is not of this world" (John 18:36).

With those words, Jesus reversed the expectation for the Messiah-King—instead of coming as a powerful worldly ruler, establishing a kingdom for himself through violence, he came as a humble man from a small village, and he established the kingdom of God through his Paschal Mystery: suffering and dying on the Cross to rise again.

Pilate, recognizing that Jesus didn't seek an earthly throne, offered to release Jesus, but the chief priests stirred up the crowd to call for Jesus to be crucified and for Barabbas to be released instead. So, to placate the crowds and prevent a violent revolt, Pilate had Jesus scourged and gave him to the soldiers to be crucified.

All Sinners Were the Authors of Christ's Passion

The events of Jesus' arrest and trial were complex and involved several different groups. Jesus' own followers betrayed and abandoned him, a group of Jewish leaders convicted him of blasphemy and accused him before Pilate of opposing Caesar (Luke 23:2), and the Roman authorities scourged him and subjected him to the cruelest execution.

While the Gospel of John sometimes refers to the crowd that had been stirred up against Jesus as simply "the Jews," it's important to recognize that not all Jews at the time of Jesus consented to the condemnation of Jesus. Jesus and his disciples were Jews themselves, and Jesus even had followers among the religious leadership (John 12:42). Those who did take part in condemning Jesus didn't know or believe that he was the Son of God, so they didn't fully understand what they were doing. Jesus acknowledged this when he prayed for them on the Cross, saying, "Father, forgive them; for they know not what they do" (Luke 23:34; see also Acts 3:17; 1 Cor 2:8). Therefore, it's a mistake to lay blame on the Jewish people as a whole—at Jesus' time or at any time—for the death of Jesus (CCC 595–597).

Jesus died to save us all from our sins. Thus, all of us, as sinners, are responsible for the death of Jesus. In fact, we Christians, who know Jesus and know why he died yet continue to offend him with our sins, are in a certain sense more responsible than the people of Jerusalem at the time of Jesus, who acted in ignorance (CCC 598).

The Crucifixion and Death of Jesus

Assigned Reading
Mark 15:16–47

After taking Jesus from Pilate, the soldiers mocked Jesus' kingship and then led him out to Golgotha to crucify him. They offered him wine mixed with myrrh—a painkiller—but he refused it, choosing to drink fully the cup of suffering he accepted in the garden. They nailed him to the Cross and divided his garments, fulfilling what was written in Psalm 22:18. Likewise, on the Cross hung an inscription detailing the charge against him. It mockingly proclaimed, "The King of the Jews." The passersby and the chief priests also mocked Jesus and taunted him with the accusation they made before the council that he would tear down the temple and rebuild it in three days.

Darkness came over the land at noon ("the sixth hour"), and then at three in the afternoon ("the ninth hour"), Jesus cried out, "My God, my God, why have you forsaken me?" (Mark 15:34). He gave one last cry and died. At that moment, the curtain in the temple tore in two—symbolizing both the end of the Old Testament worship and the end of the division between God and man. In the same moment, a centurion (a Roman commander of 100 soldiers), after witnessing how Jesus died, exclaimed, "Truly this man was the Son of God!" (Mark 15:39).

Jesus, the Suffering Servant

The events of Jesus' Passion fulfilled Isaiah's prophecy, made hundreds of years earlier, about the Suffering Servant (Isa 52:13–53:12). Let's reread this prophecy and examine it in detail in light of the events of Jesus' Passion.

> **Assigned Reading**
> Isaiah 52:13–53:12

Isaiah 53:3

He was despised and rejected by men;
a man of sorrows, and acquainted with grief;

Jesus was despised and rejected by the crowd. His claim to kingship was scorned and mocked. Even his closest followers deserted him and hid.

Isaiah 53:4

. . . we esteemed him stricken,
struck down by God, and afflicted.

The chief priests and crowd saw Jesus' Crucifixion as a judgment from God, disproving his claim to be the Messiah and the King of the Jews.

Isaiah 53:5

But he was wounded for our transgressions,
he was bruised for our iniquities;

In reality, his suffering was the consequence of our sin, and it brings us redemption. All of us have gone astray through sin; but, by his suffering, we are healed.

Isaiah 53:7

yet he opened not his mouth;
like a lamb that is led to the slaughter,

Isaiah compares the servant to a lamb led to the slaughter. John the Baptist declared that Jesus is "the Lamb of God, who takes away the sin of the world" (John 1:29). Jesus is the Paschal Lamb, who was silent before those who accused him falsely. His sacrifice on the Cross fulfills what the Passover prefigured. His Blood delivers us from slavery to sin and death (see Part II, Chapter 2).

Isaiah 53:8–9

. . . he was cut off out of the land of the living,
. . . And they made his grave with the wicked
and with a rich man in his death.

Jesus suffered death—he was cut off from the land of the living. He was without sin and did not resist with violence, but he was executed like a wicked criminal beside other criminals, and he was buried in a tomb belonging to a rich man—Joseph of Arimathea (Matt 27:57–60).

Isaiah 53:10

Yet it was the will of the Lord to bruise him; . . .
he shall see his offspring, he shall prolong his days;

Jesus' suffering and death did not happen by chance, but was the culmination of the Father's plan of salvation. Though he had been cut off from the land of the living, his death was not the end: "he shall see his offspring, he shall prolong his days." In other words, he will live!

The Mystery of Redemptive Love and Suffering

Isaiah's prophecy helps us see that the suffering and death of Jesus was not a meaningless accident, but rather a part of God's plan to redeem humanity. This doesn't mean that God caused Jesus' death himself or that Judas or the chief priests acted like puppets, but that God foresaw the evil choices they would make freely and permitted them so that he could bring something good out of them (CCC 599–600). As Jesus himself explained to his disciples, his suffering and death was part of God's plan of salvation foretold in Isaiah 53 and throughout the Old Testament (Luke 24:25–27; CCC 601).

How, though, is it possible that our salvation can come out of something as terrible as the cruel execution of Jesus, the Son of God?

While our redemption through the Cross is a mystery of faith that we can never fully comprehend, Scripture gives us a few concepts that provide some understanding of how this can be.

The first of these is the idea of "redemption" or "ransom." We use the terms "redeem" and "redemption" in reference to our salvation by Jesus so often that we can forget the words' original meaning. "To redeem" means, literally, to buy back; and, specifically, it means to pay a price to release someone from slavery or captivity. Likewise, a "ransom" is the price paid to free someone from captivity. (And, as a verb, "to ransom" means the same thing as "to redeem.") The First Letter of St. Peter says that we were ransomed by the Blood of Christ:

> You know that you were ransomed from the futile ways inherited from your fathers, not with perishable things such as silver or gold, but with the precious blood of Christ, like that of a lamb without blemish or spot. He was destined before the foundation of the world but was made manifest at the end of the times for your sake. Through him you have confidence in God, who raised him from the dead and gave him glory, so that your faith and hope are in God. (1 Peter 1:18–21)

As we learned from Genesis, the consequence of sin is death. After the original sin of our first parents, we were slaves to sin and death, but on the Cross, Jesus bore the consequence of our sin. Even though he didn't sin himself, he united himself to us in our separation from God so deeply that he could cry out in our name, "My God, my God, why have you forsaken me?" (Mark 15:34) and could suffer the death that we deserved because of our sins. This was the price paid to "buy us back" from our slavery. Our freedom was purchased with the blood of Christ, which is more precious than silver, gold, or anything else that we could offer (CCC 602–603).

An Offering to the Father

The second concept necessary for understanding how Jesus redeems us on the Cross is the idea of "sacrifice." Throughout human history, human beings have offered sacrifice to God as expiation for sin—giving something of value back to God to make up for our guilt.

Sacrifice for sin was part of the Law of Moses, but as the Letter to the Hebrews explains, the "blood of bulls and goats" (which were offered for sin under the Law of Moses) couldn't take away sins (Heb 10:4). Such sacrifices could foreshadow the sacrifice of Jesus. They could help people see how incapable they were, on their own, of truly atoning for sin. But that was it. There was a limit to their efficacy.

The author of Hebrews then goes on to quote Psalm 40:6–8, attributing the words to Christ.

> Sacrifice and offering you do not desire;
> but you have given me an open ear.
> Burnt offering and sin offering
> you have not required.
> Then I said, "Behold, I come;
> in the roll of the book it is written of me;
> I delight to do your will, O my God;
> your law is within my heart."

These words tells us that God does not ultimately desire animal sacrifices. What he desires is obedience. What he desires is the response of Jesus: "I have come to do your will."

In perfect obedience to the will of the Father, Jesus offered up his body on the Cross. Because Jesus is fully God and fully man, his total offering of himself in obedience had the power to make up for our sins—unlike all the sacrifices that came before it. It was a gift from God the Father himself, because he handed his Son over to reconcile us to himself, and it was the sacrifice of the Son, who, incarnate as a man, offered himself to the Father in obedience. As the Suffering Servant, he substituted his obedience for our disobedience, and this obedience in love redeems us and makes us righteous (Isa 53:11; CCC 614–615).

> It is love "to the end" [*Jn* 13:1] that confers on Christ's sacrifice its value as redemption and reparation, as atonement and satisfaction. He knew and loved us all when he offered his life [Cf. *Gal* 2:20; *Eph* 5:2, 25]. Now "the love of Christ controls us, because we are convinced that one has died for all; therefore all have died" [2 *Cor* 5:14]. No man, not even the holiest, was ever able to take on himself the sins of all men and offer himself as a sacrifice for all. The existence in Christ of the divine person of the Son, who at once surpasses and embraces all human persons and constitutes himself as the Head of all mankind, makes possible his redemptive sacrifice for all. (CCC 616)

The Paschal Sacrifice: The Lamb of God

Jesus' whole life was an offering to the Father. From the first moment of his Incarnation, he embraced the Father's plan of salvation—he came to serve and to offer his life as ransom for us (Mark 10:45). Out of love for the Father and for us, he freely accepted his Passion and death on the Cross "like a lamb that is led to the slaughter" (Isa 53:7), and so became "the free and perfect instrument of his divine love which desires the salvation of men [Cf. *Heb* 2:10,17–18; 4:15; 5:7–9]" (CCC 609). As John the

Baptist said, he is the "Lamb of God, who takes away the sin of the world" (John 1:29; CCC 606–608).

As the Lamb of God, Jesus is the fulfillment of the sacrifice of the Passover—God's ultimate act of deliverance in the Old Testament. At the Passover, every household sacrificed an unblemished lamb and smeared its blood on their doorposts and was thus delivered from death and slavery. On the Cross, Jesus, the Lamb of God, offered himself as the Paschal sacrifice. By his blood, poured out in love and smeared on the wood of the Cross, we are delivered from death and slavery to sin.

We Participate in Christ's Sacrifice

Jesus is the "one mediator between God and men" (1 Tim 2:5), and his sacrifice is the unique source of our eternal salvation. However, we are united to him through his Incarnation and in the Church in a way that makes it possible for us to act as his partners in the work of redemption. In the Gospels he calls his disciples to take up their own cross and follow him (Matt 16:24), and he associates the suffering his first disciples would endure with his own. The Apostles, he tells us, are to drink the cup he drinks (Mark 10:39). All Christians who do so, St. Paul adds, complete what is lacking in Christ's sufferings with their own sufferings for the sake of the Church (Col 1:24). In this, Mary, who was more closely associated with the mystery of Christ's suffering than any other person, is our ultimate example (Luke 2:35; CCC 618).

Like Mary and the Apostles, we are to unite our entire lives to the suffering of Christ. We are to take up our own cross and lay down our own lives for others, following the example of Jesus.

In his Letter to the Philippians, St. Paul described the attitude we are supposed to have by detailing Christ's offering of himself in words that recalled Isaiah's prophecy of the Suffering Servant (Phil 2:6–11). Christ Jesus is the eternal Son of God, but for our salvation, he "emptied himself."

Rather than clinging to his divine glory or exploiting it, he took up the lowliness of our human condition and came to us as a servant (Phil 2:6–7). He humbled himself and was obedient to the Father to the point of enduring death—and not just any death, but the worst kind of death:

the cruel, humiliating, execution of a criminal on the Cross (Phil 2:8). Jesus emptied himself to share his glory with us. He became poor so that we might become rich (2 Cor 8:9), and he suffered in our place so that by his obedience we might regain what we lost by our disobedience. "Upon him was the chastisement that made us whole" (Isa 53:5). But death is not the end of the Servant. Because of his obedience, God will glorify him so that all creation will confess that he is Lord (Phil 2:9–11).

SELECTED READING

Pope St. John Paul II, Encyclical Letter on the Eucharist in Its Relationship to the Church *Ecclesia de Eucharistia* (April 17, 2003), nos. 2–4

Did the Apostles who took part in the Last Supper understand the meaning of the words spoken by Christ? Perhaps not. Those words would only be fully clear at the end of the *Triduum sacrum*, the time from Thursday evening to Sunday morning. Those days embrace the *mysterium paschale*; they also embrace the *mysterium eucharisticum*.

The Church was born of the paschal mystery. For this very reason the Eucharist, which is in an outstanding way the sacrament of the paschal mystery, *stands at the centre of the Church's life*. This is already clear from the earliest images of the Church found in the Acts of the Apostles: "They devoted themselves to the Apostles' teaching and fellowship, to the breaking of bread and the prayers" (2:42). The "breaking of the bread" refers to the Eucharist. Two thousand years later, we continue to relive that primordial image of the Church. At every celebration of the Eucharist, we are spiritually brought back to the paschal Triduum: to the events of the evening of Holy Thursday, to the Last Supper and to what followed it. The institution of the Eucharist sacramentally anticipated the events which were about to take place, beginning with the agony in Gethsemane. Once again we see Jesus as he leaves the Upper Room, descends with his disciples to the Kidron valley and goes to the Garden of Olives. Even today that Garden shelters some very ancient olive trees. Perhaps they witnessed what happened beneath their shade that evening, when Christ in prayer was filled with anguish "and his sweat became like drops of blood falling down upon the ground" (cf. *Lk* 22:44). The blood which shortly before he had given to the Church as the drink of salvation in the sacrament of the Eucharist, *began to be shed*; its outpouring would then be completed on Golgotha to become the means of our redemption: "Christ . . . as high priest of the good things to come . . . , entered once for all into the Holy Place, taking not the blood of goats and calves but his own blood, thus securing an eternal redemption" (*Heb* 9:11–12).

The hour of our redemption. Although deeply troubled, Jesus does not flee before his "hour." "And what shall I say? 'Father, save me from this hour?' No, for this purpose I have come to this hour" (*Jn* 12:27). He wanted his disciples to keep him company, yet he had to experience loneliness and abandonment: "So, could you not watch with me one hour? Watch and pray that you may not enter into temptation" (*Mt* 26:40–41). Only John would remain at the foot of the Cross, at the side of Mary and the faithful women. The agony in Gethsemane was the introduction to the agony of the Cross on Good Friday. *The holy hour,* the hour of the redemption of the world. Whenever the Eucharist is celebrated at the tomb of Jesus in Jerusalem, there is an almost tangible return to his "hour," the hour of his Cross and glorification. Every priest who celebrates Holy Mass, together with the Christian community which takes part in it, is led back in spirit to that place and that hour.

QUESTIONS FOR REVIEW

1. Who was responsible for Jesus' death?
2. What prophecy of Isaiah's did Jesus' Passion and death fulfill?
3. On the Cross, what did Jesus accomplish?
4. How does the concept of "ransom" help us understand Jesus' death?
5. How does the concept of "offering" or "sacrifice" help us understand Jesus' death?

QUESTIONS FOR DISCUSSION

1. Why is it easier to blame others for Jesus' death than it is to see how we, too, are responsible for it?
2. Jesus showed us how much he loves us by offering up his life for us. What does this teach you about love and greatness?
3. St. Paul teaches us that when we humbly accept our trials without complaint and unite them in prayer to Jesus' sufferings, they become a means of grace and redemption for others. What is one suffering you could "offer up" for someone else? Do you have someone specific in mind?

Chapter 2

The Resurrection of Jesus

Christ Descended into Hell

Jesus experienced death fully, like all human beings, and in his soul he joined those in the realm of the dead. In the Apostles' Creed, we confess that Jesus "descended into hell." "Hell," in this case, does not refer to the hell of the damned but rather to the dwelling place of the dead (*sheol* in Hebrew or *hades* in Greek), where the souls of the just waited for the redeemer. To those in *sheol,* Jesus came as savior—freeing them from death and allowing them to share in the vision of God in heaven (CCC 631–633).

By descending to the dead and freeing the souls of the just who died before him, Jesus brought the Gospel message to complete fulfillment, bringing his redemption to people of all times and places. Now, the risen Christ reigns over all creation—heaven and earth, visible and invisible (Phil 2:9–11). He conquered the devil and the power of death, to deliver us from fear of death (Heb 2:14–15; CCC 634–635).

On the Third Day, He Rose from the Dead

On the third day—that is, the Sunday following the Friday on which he died—Jesus rose again from the grave. The Resurrection of Jesus is "the crowning truth of our faith in Christ" and "an essential part of the Paschal Mystery along with the cross" (CCC 638).

Assigned Reading
Mark 16:1–20

A Historical Event

The accounts in Mark and the other Gospels affirm that the Resurrection of Jesus was a real, historical event, which was verified by witnesses. The first sign that Jesus had risen was the empty tomb. This wasn't direct proof of the Resurrection—the Gospel of Matthew records that the chief priests attempted to spread a story that the disciples had stolen the body (Matt 28:11–15)—but its discovery by the disciples was their first step toward recognizing the Resurrection (CCC 640).

Jesus then confirmed what had happened by appearing to his disciples. He first appeared to Mary Magdalene and the holy women who had come to anoint his body, which they presumed would be there. They were the first messengers of the good news of the Resurrection—bringing word to the Apostles. The Apostles, however, were still mourning Jesus' death and didn't believe the women until he appeared to them as well. The Gospels record several of these appearances to the Apostles and other disciples. These appearances and everything that occurred in the days after Jesus' death and Resurrection prepared the Apostles for the work of spreading the Good News and building up the Church. As the primary witnesses to Jesus' Resurrection, they are the foundation stones of the Church. Importantly, though, they were not the only witnesses. St. Paul speaks of the witness of more than five hundred people:

> For I delivered to you as of first importance what I also received, that Christ died for our sins in accordance with the Scriptures, that he was buried, that he was raised on the third day in accordance with the Scriptures, and that he appeared to Ce'phas [that is, Peter], then to the Twelve. Then he appeared to more than five hundred brethren at one time, most of whom are still alive,

> though some have fallen asleep. Then he appeared to James, then to all the apostles. Last of all, as to one untimely born, he appeared also to me. (1 Cor 15:3–8)

The faith of the first Christians in the Resurrection was based on the witness of these men and women who lived among them (CCC 641–642).

Some people have attempted to explain Jesus' Resurrection as a purely spiritual event brought about by the faith of the Apostles. However, the accounts of the Apostles and other witnesses clearly testify that Jesus' Resurrection was a historical, physical event: the tomb was empty and Jesus walked among us, touched us, and ate with us. When the women brought the news to the Apostles, they were demoralized and didn't believe it; so it can't be the case that their faith brought about a purely mystical experience of the Resurrection. On the contrary, their direct encounter with the risen Lord gave rise to their faith (CCC 643–644).

A Transcendent Event

Jesus proved to the disciples that he was not a ghost. He touched them and ate with them and showed them that his risen body was the same body that was crucified (Luke 24:30, 39–40, 41–43; John 20:20, 27; 21:9, 13). At the same time, Jesus' risen body is glorified and is no longer limited by space and time—he can be present wherever and however he wills. For instance, he was able to enter the room where the Apostles were hiding, even though the doors were closed. When he appeared to Mary Magdalene, she didn't recognize him until he addressed her by name (John 20:14–16, 26; CCC 645). Jesus didn't just return to earthly life like Lazarus and the other people he raised from the dead. They would die again someday, but Jesus rose to another life, beyond time and space, and his body is filled with the power of the Holy Spirit (CCC 646).

No one witnessed the actual event of his rising from the dead, and the Gospels don't describe it, so we don't know precisely how it came about physically or what it was like for him to pass over to a new kind of life. So, while the historical reality of Jesus' Resurrection was verified by the empty tomb and the appearances he made, it remains a mystery of faith that transcends history.

The Significance of the Resurrection

The Resurrection confirms the truth of Jesus' divinity. It shows us that he truly is the Son of God and God himself, who came with divine authority. It confirms everything he did and taught and justifies our belief in him and the mysteries of the faith revealed by him. Jesus himself said, "When you lift up the Son of Man, then you will realize that I AM, and that I do nothing on my own, but I say only what the Father taught me" (John 8:28, NABRE). In other words, the Resurrection reveals who Jesus really is, and he is "I AM," which is the meaning of the name of God revealed to Moses (Exod 3:14). It shows that, as the Son of God, Jesus has authority over death: "I have power to lay [my life] down, and I have power to take it again" (John 10:18). Moreover, it confirms that everything he did and said was done with this divine authority: "I do nothing on my own, but I say only what the Father taught me." Because Jesus taught with this authority, we can trust that his teaching is true. Thus, all the truths of our faith, even those that we can't fully grasp or prove by reason alone, are confirmed by the Resurrection (CCC 651, 653).

The Resurrection likewise fulfills the promises made in the Old Testament and Jesus' own predictions. During his ministry, Jesus had foretold his own death and Resurrection several times. He told Peter, James, and John not to tell anyone about his Transfiguration until after he had risen from the dead (Mark 9:9–10), and when the people asked for a sign, he told them, "Destroy this temple, and in three days I will raise it up" (John 2:19), speaking of the temple of his body.

After the Resurrection, the meaning of these predictions became clear to the disciples, and Jesus explained to them how his death and Resurrection were foretold in the Old Testament: "Then he opened their minds to understand the Scriptures, and said to them, 'Thus it is written, that the Christ should suffer and on the third day rise from the dead'" (Luke 24:45–46). We already learned how Isaiah prophesied that the Lord's Servant who was "cut off from the land of the living" would yet live (Isa 53:8–10; see "Jesus, the Suffering Servant" in Part IV, Chapter 1). We can also see the Resurrection foreshadowed in the words of Psalm 16:10–11 (see also Acts 13:35) and in the story of Jonah: "For as Jonah was three days and three nights in the belly of the whale, so will the Son of man be three days and three nights in the heart of the earth" (Matt 12:40; see Jonah 2:1). As we profess in the Nicene Creed, Jesus was raised "in accordance with the Scriptures" (CCC 651–653).

Jesus' Resurrection is the second aspect of his Paschal Mystery. The first aspect is his suffering and death on the Cross. By this he freed us from sin. By the second aspect, his Resurrection, he opens the way to a new life for us. Through our Baptism we share in his victory over death, which was caused by sin, so we are freed from fear of it and we are reinstated in the friendship and grace of God. This is called justification. It makes us adopted children of God so that we become brothers and sisters of Christ, sharing in his life (CCC 654).

Finally, Jesus' Resurrection is the source and promise of our own future resurrection. Jesus is "the first fruits of those who have fallen asleep" (1 Cor 15:20). His victory over death makes our resurrection possible and confirms his promise that, when he returns in glory, we shall be raised from the dead like he was (CCC 655).

We Participate in the Mystery of Redemption through the Sacraments

We take part in the Paschal Mystery through the sacraments. For example, St. Paul tells us that in Baptism, we are joined to Jesus' death and Resurrection:

> Do you not know that all of us who have been baptized into Christ Jesus were baptized into his death? We were buried therefore with him by baptism into death, so that as Christ was raised from the dead by the glory of the Father, we too might walk in newness of life. (Rom 6:3–4)

Above all, though, we participate in the Paschal Mystery through the Eucharist. At the Last Supper, Jesus transformed the bread and wine of the Passover meal into his own Body and Blood, which would be offered and poured out on Good Friday and raised from the dead on Easter Sunday. He commanded his Apostles to perpetuate this as a memorial of his sacrifice, making them the first priests of the New Covenant. This memorial doesn't just recall the events of Jesus' Passover but actually makes them present and real.

As at the Last Supper, Jesus makes his Paschal Mystery present at every Mass. His sacrificial death on the Cross is unique and unrepeatable, so the Mass is not a new sacrifice, much less is it a repetition of Jesus' death. Rather, the sacrifice of Christ on the Cross and the sacrifice of the Mass are the same sacrifice. At the consecration, bread and wine become Jesus' Body and Blood—the same Body and Blood that he offered to the Father for our sins on the Cross and which the Father raised up on the third day. Thus, the Eucharist makes the one sacrifice of Christ present to the Church in every age. It allows us to unite our own lives—our praise, suffering, prayer, and work—with his offering on the Cross (CCC 1365–1368).

SELECTED READING

Pope St. John Paul II, Encyclical Letter *Dives in Misericordia* (November 30, 1980), no. 8

The cross of Christ on Calvary is also a witness to the strength of evil against the very Son of God, against the one who, alone among all the sons of men, was by His nature absolutely innocent and free from sin, and whose coming into the world was untainted by the disobedience of Adam and the inheritance of original sin. And here, precisely in Him, in Christ, justice is done to sin at the price of His sacrifice, of His obedience "even to death," He who was without sin, "God made him sin for our sake." Justice is also brought to bear upon death, which from the beginning of man's history had been allied to sin. Death has justice done to it at the price of the death of the one who was without sin and who alone was able—by means of his own death—to inflict death upon death. In this way the cross of Christ, on which the Son, consubstantial with the Father, renders full justice to God, is also a radical revelation of mercy, or rather of the love that goes against what constitutes the very root of evil in the history of man: against sin and death.

The cross is the most profound condescension of God to man and to what man—especially in difficult and painful moments—looks on as his unhappy destiny. The cross is like a touch of eternal love upon the most painful wounds of man's earthly existence; it is the total fulfillment of the messianic program that Christ once formulated in the synagogue at Nazareth and then repeated to the messengers sent by John the Baptist. According to the words once written in the prophecy of Isaiah, this program consisted in the revelation of merciful love for the poor, the suffering and prisoners, for the blind, the oppressed and sinners. In the paschal mystery the limits of the many sided evil in which man becomes a sharer during his earthly existence are surpassed: the cross of Christ, in fact, makes us understand the deepest roots of evil, which are fixed in sin and death; thus the cross becomes an eschatological sign. Only in the eschatological fulfillment and definitive renewal of the world will love conquer, in all the elect, the deepest sources of evil, bringing as its fully mature fruit the kingdom of life and holiness and glorious immortality. The foundation of this eschatological fulfillment is already contained in the cross of Christ and in His death. The fact that Christ "was raised the third day" constitutes the final sign of the messianic mission, a sign that perfects the entire revelation of merciful love in a world that is subject to evil. At the same time it constitutes the sign that foretells "a new heaven and a new earth," when God "will wipe away every tear from their eyes, there will be no more death, or mourning no crying, nor pain, for the former things have passed away."

In the eschatological fulfillment mercy will be revealed as love, while in the temporal phase, in human history, which is at the same time the history of sin and death, love must be revealed above all as mercy and must also be actualized as mercy. Christ's messianic program, the program of mercy, becomes the program of His people, the program of the Church. At its very center there is always the cross, for it is in the cross that the revelation of merciful love attains its culmination. Until "the former things pass away," the cross will remain the point of reference for other words too of the Revelation of John: "Behold, I stand at the door and knock; if anyone hears my voice and opens the door, I will come in and eat with him and he with me." In a special way, God also reveals His mercy when He invites man to have "mercy" on His only Son, the crucified one.

Christ, precisely as the crucified one, is the Word that does not pass away, and He is the one who stands at the door and knocks at the heart of every man, without restricting his freedom, but instead seeking to draw from this very freedom love, which is not only an act of solidarity with the suffering Son of man, but also a kind of "mercy" shown by each one of us to the Son of the eternal Father. In the whole of this messianic program of Christ, in the whole revelation of mercy through the cross, could man's dignity be more highly respected and ennobled, for, in obtaining mercy, He is in a sense the one who at the same time "shows mercy"? In a word, is not this the position of Christ with regard to man when He says: "As you did it to one of the least of these . . . you did it to me?" Do not the words of the Sermon on the Mount: "Blessed are the merciful, for they shall obtain mercy," constitute, in a certain sense, a synthesis of the whole of the Good News, of the whole of the "wonderful exchange" (*admirable commercium*) contained therein? This exchange is a law of the very plan of salvation, a law which is simple, strong and at the same time "easy." Demonstrating from the very start what the "human heart" is capable of ("to be merciful"), do not these words from the Sermon on the Mount reveal in the same perspective the deep mystery of God: that inscrutable unity of Father, Son and Holy Spirit, in which love, containing justice, sets in motion mercy, which in its turn reveals the perfection of justice?

The Paschal Mystery is Christ at the summit of the revelation of the inscrutable mystery of God. It is precisely then that the words pronounced in the Upper Room are completely fulfilled: "He who has seen me has seen the Father." In fact, Christ, whom the Father "did not spare" for the sake of man and who in His passion and in the torment of the cross did not obtain human mercy, has revealed in His resurrection the fullness of the love that the Father has for Him and, in Him, for all people. "He is not God of the dead, but of the living." In His resurrection Christ has revealed the God of merciful love, precisely because He accepted the cross as the way to the resurrection. And it is for this reason that—when we recall the cross of Christ, His passion and death—our faith and hope are centered on the Risen One: on that Christ who "on the evening of that day, the first day of the week, . . . stood among them" in the upper Room, "where the disciples were, . . . breathed on them, and said to them: 'Receive the Holy Spirit. If you forgive the sins of any, they are forgiven; if you retain the sins of any, they are retained.'"

Here is the Son of God, who in His resurrection experienced in a radical way mercy shown to Himself, that is to say the love of the Father which is more powerful than death. And it is also the same Christ, the Son of God, who at the end of His messianic mission—and, in a certain sense, even beyond the end—reveals Himself as the inexhaustible source of mercy, of the same love that, in a subsequent perspective of the history of salvation in the Church, is to be everlastingly confirmed as more powerful than sin. The paschal Christ is the definitive incarnation of mercy, its living sign in salvation history and in eschatology. In the same spirit, the liturgy of Eastertide places on our lips the words of the Psalm: *Misericordias Domini in aeternum cantabo*.

QUESTIONS FOR REVIEW

1. What is *sheol* and what did Jesus do there?
2. After his Resurrection, to whom did Jesus first appear?
3. What is the significance of Jesus' Resurrection?
4. What are the two aspects of the Paschal Mystery?
5. How do we participate in the Paschal Mystery?

QUESTIONS FOR DISCUSSION

1. If we stay close to Jesus all our lives, after the final judgment, we, too, will have glorified bodies, like him. To what aspect of having a glorified body are you most looking forward?
2. When it comes to death, of what are you most afraid? Does knowledge of Jesus and his Resurrection lessen that fear? Why or why not?
3. How can you take better advantage of the graces offered to you in the sacraments?

Chapter 3

The Ascension of Jesus into Heaven

Assigned Reading
Acts 1:1–11

Forty days after the Resurrection, the Apostles witnessed the entry of Jesus' humanity into divine glory as he ascended into the heavens and disappeared into a cloud—a symbol of God's presence and glory.

The Ascension fulfills Jesus' words to the chief priests: "you will see the Son of man sitting at the right hand of Power, and coming with the clouds of heaven" (Mark 14:62), and the prophecy of Daniel concerning the Son of Man:

> I saw in the night visions,
> and behold, with the clouds of heaven
> there came one like a son of man,
> and he came to the Ancient of Days
> and was presented before him.
> And to him was given dominion
> and glory and kingdom,
> that all peoples, nations, and languages
> should serve him;

> his dominion is an everlasting dominion,
> which shall not pass away,
> and his kingdom one
> that shall not be destroyed. (Dan 7:13–14)

Now, for all eternity, Jesus sits at the right hand of the Father, not only as our king, but also as our high priest. He leads the heavenly worship that honors the Father, and he intercedes for us with the Father: "For Christ has entered, not into a sanctuary made with hands, a copy of the true one, but into heaven itself, now to appear in the presence of God on our behalf" (Heb 9:24; CCC 662).

"You Shall Receive Power"

Jesus ascended into heaven to begin his reign in glory, but he didn't abandon us. On the contrary, he said, "I am with you always, to the close of the age" (Matt 28:20). Jesus remains with his Church in many ways. He is present and at work in the sacraments, especially the Eucharist. He is present in the Gospel handed on through Scripture and Tradition. He is present in the successors of the Apostles, who teach and exercise authority in his name. And he is present whenever believers gather in his name, for he says, "For where two or three are gathered in my name, there am I in the midst of them" (Matt 18:20).

Moreover, not only does Jesus remain present to us, but so too does the Holy Spirit, whom, at the Last Supper, he first promised to send to us: "I will ask the Father, and he will give you another Counselor, to be with you for ever, even the Spirit of truth" (John 14:16–17). Later, before ascending to heaven, he told his Apostles to wait for the coming of the Spirit, who would give them power to be his witnesses to the end of the earth (Acts 1:4–5, 8). That promise was fulfilled on the feast of Pentecost, when the Holy Spirit descended upon the Apostles, who were gathered in the Upper Room with the Blessed Virgin Mary (Acts 2:1–42).

On that day, the Apostles were transformed by the power of the Holy Spirit. The same men who had abandoned and denied Jesus during his

Passion and then went into hiding out of fear were filled with courage. From the Spirit they received the words to testify to the good news of Jesus' victory over sin and death throughout the known world. They also received the power to work miracles and the strength to witness to Jesus even to the point of suffering death themselves.

Jesus' intercession for us in heaven assures us that the Holy Spirit continues to be poured out upon the Church. It is the Holy Spirit who makes Jesus present in the sacraments (CCC 667). It is the Holy Spirit who inspired the Scriptures and who continues to guide the Church in her teaching and preservation of the Deposit of Faith. And it is the Holy Spirit who comes into each one of our hearts, giving us the power to profess faith in Jesus and acknowledge God as our Father: "God has sent the Spirit of his Son into our hearts, crying, 'Abba! Father!'" (Gal 4:6).

We Will Follow Where He Has Gone Before

Jesus' ascension into heaven completed the mission of his earthly life, which began with his Incarnation. As members of his Body, the Church, we hope to follow where Jesus, the Head of the Church, has gone:

> He ascended, not to distance himself from our lowly state
> but that we, his members, might be confident of following
> where he, our Head and Founder, has gone before.[1]

In heaven, Jesus has prepared a place for us (John 14:2). If we die in friendship with him, our souls will join him in heaven, and when he returns in glory, our bodies will also be raised up. They will be glorified like his and, like him, we will share, body and soul, in the joy and glory of heaven (CCC 661).

---

[1] "Preface of the Ascension," in *The Roman Missal: Renewed by Decree of the Most Holy Second Ecumenical Council of the Vatican, Promulgated by Authority of Pope Paul VI and Revised at the Direction of Pope John Paul II*, third typical edition (hereafter cited as Order of Mass) (Washington DC: United States Conference of Catholic Bishops, 2011), 50.

Right now, however, Jesus' mother Mary already shares in that glory, in both body and soul. No human being is closer to Jesus than his mother, Mary. Mary was preserved from all sin to prepare the way for Jesus, and she shared in his earthly life, from the first moment of his Incarnation to his Passion and death. Therefore, at the end of her life, Jesus preserved her from the decay of death that results from sin and took her, body and soul, to be with him in heaven (CCC 966).

Mary is the Mother of the Church. Her closeness to Jesus continues in heaven and she helps the Church with her prayers there, just as she did in the days after Jesus' Ascension (Acts 1:14). Mary's intercession, however, is distinct from the unique intercession of Jesus. Jesus is the one mediator between God and man, but he allows us to cooperate in his work of redemption and priestly intercession. Thus, the intercession of Mary, of the saints in heaven, and of Christians on earth who pray for each other depends entirely upon Jesus (CCC 969–970).

Mary's special role and her preservation from sin and death come from Jesus and point us back to him. She is our model of how to follow him. As his first and preeminent disciple, she is a "type" of the Church itself—that is, she is a perfect example that shows us, like a pattern or model, what the Church as a whole is and should be (CCC 967). Thus, Mary's Assumption into heaven foreshadows what Jesus will do for his entire Church. If we follow Mary's example of faith, charity, and discipleship, Jesus will raise us up to be with him just as he did for her.

SELECTED READING

Pope Benedict XVI, *Reflections on the Ascension of Our Lord*, Homily, May 7, 2005

So what does the Feast of the Ascension of the Lord mean for us? It does not mean that the Lord has departed to some place far from people and from the world. Christ's Ascension is not a journey into space toward the most remote stars; for basically, the planets, like the earth, are also made of physical elements.

Christ's Ascension means that he no longer belongs to the world of corruption and death that conditions our life. It means that he belongs entirely to God. He, the Eternal Son, led our human existence into God's presence, taking with him flesh and blood in a transfigured form.

The human being finds room in God; through Christ, the human being was introduced into the very life of God. And since God embraces and sustains the entire cosmos, the Ascension of the Lord means that Christ has not departed from us, but that he is now, thanks to his being with the Father, close to each one of us for ever. Each one of us can be on intimate terms with him; each can call upon him. The Lord is always within hearing. We can inwardly draw away from him. We can live turning our backs on him. But he always waits for us and is always close to us.

From the readings of today's liturgy we also learn something more about the concrete way the Lord makes himself close to us. The Lord promises the disciples his Holy Spirit. The first reading that we heard tells us that the Holy Spirit will give "power" to the disciples; the Gospel adds that he will guide them to the whole truth. As the living Word of God, Jesus told his disciples everything, and God can give no more than himself. In Jesus, God gave us his whole self, that is, he gave us everything. As well as or together with this, there can be no other revelation which can communicate more or in some way complete the Revelation of Christ. In him, in the Son, all has been said to us, all has been given.

But our understanding is limited: thus, the Spirit's mission is to introduce the Church, in an ever new way from generation to generation, into the greatness of Christ's mystery. The Spirit places nothing different or new beside Christ; no pneumatic revelation comes with the revelation of Christ—as some say—no second level of Revelation.

No: "He will have received from me . . . ," Christ says in the Gospel (Jn 16:14). And as Christ says only what he hears and receives from the Father, thus the Holy Spirit is the interpreter of Christ. "He will have received from me." He does not lead us to other places, far from Christ, but takes us further and further into Christ's

> light. Consequently, Christian Revelation is both ever old and new. Thus, all things are and always have been given to us. At the same time, every generation, in the inexhaustible encounter with the Lord—an encounter mediated by the Holy Spirit—always learns something new.
>
> The Holy Spirit, therefore, is the power through which Christ causes us to experience his closeness. But the first reading also has something else to say: you will be my witnesses. The Risen Christ needs witnesses who have met him, people who have known him intimately through the power of the Holy Spirit; those who have, so to speak, actually touched him, can witness to him.
>
> It is in this way that the Church, the family of Christ, "beginning at Jerusalem . . . ," as the Reading says, spread to the very ends of the earth. It is through witnesses that the Church was built—starting with Peter and Paul and the Twelve, to the point of including all who, filled with Christ, have rekindled down the centuries and will rekindle the flame of faith in a way that is ever new. All Christians in their own way can and must be witnesses of the Risen Lord.

QUESTIONS FOR REVIEW

1. How many days after the Resurrection did the Ascension occur?
2. On what feast day did the Holy Spirit descend upon the Apostles?
3. What is the Holy Spirit's relationship to the sacraments?
4. Who is the Mother of the Church?
5. Upon whose power does the efficacy of Mary's prayers for us depend?

QUESTIONS FOR DISCUSSION

1. Do you ever pray to the Holy Spirit? Why or why not?
2. What is one way you can follow Mary's example?
3. What are some of the things you ask your own mother to help you with? What are some of the things you could ask Mary to help you with?

Part V

The Paschal Mystery and the Life of the Believer

Jesus won salvation for us through the Paschal Mystery of his suffering, death, and Resurrection. Now that we've studied how this mystery of our faith affects our understanding of creation, sin, the mission of Jesus, and God's entire plan of salvation, we can turn to the moral implications of this mystery. In other words, we can look at how our belief in Jesus and his mission affects the way we live our lives.

Chapter 1

Jesus Died for Our Sins and Was Raised for Our Justification

In the Nicene Creed, we profess that Jesus came "for us men and our salvation," and that he was crucified "for our sake." Jesus' mission is our salvation and his entire life is a mystery of redemption (see Part II, Chapter 3).

This mission culminates in the Paschal Mystery of his suffering, death, and Resurrection. Jesus "was put to death for our trespasses and raised for our justification" (Rom 4:25). The purpose of his death and Resurrection was to deliver us from our sins, make us holy, and restore us to friendship with God. Because of Jesus' great love for us and his tremendous gift of himself on the Cross, we can live truly joyful lives once more—not just here on earth, but forever in heaven.

There's no way we can ever repay Jesus for this. His gift to us is a gift beyond measure. Nevertheless, just recognizing the greatness of what he's done for us should motivate us to change our lives, both because we're sorry for sins and because we're grateful for the love he has shown us and want to respond in love by following his commandments (John 14:15; CCC 598).

Eternal Life—Life in Christ

Following God's commandments isn't just a matter of obeying some arbitrary set of rules so that we can obtain a future reward in heaven. And it's definitely not a question of earning salvation for ourselves by being good. We don't earn heaven like we earn privileges at home or school. We don't earn heaven at all. Eternal life is a gift beyond anything anyone can merit. God offers it to us through Jesus simply because he loves us: "God shows his love for us in that while we were yet sinners Christ died for us" (Rom 5:8). Moreover, the eternal life of heaven isn't an arbitrary reward for the life we live on earth; it is a continuation of the new life in Christ that God gives us now.

Jesus shared our human life so that we could share his divine life, and he died and rose from the dead to free us from sin and death and make us holy. This new life of holiness and friendship with God—sharing his very life—begins now. We don't have to wait until we get to heaven to enjoy it. By our Baptism we become children of God and sharers in the divine nature in this life. And through prayer and the sacraments, God offers us all the graces we need to choose his ways and his will—which are always ordered to our happiness—every day. The more time we spend with God in prayer, the more we accept the grace he offers us, and the more we make good choices—seeking to show our love for God and others in all we say and do—the more fully we participate in this new life that brings us joy (CCC 1692).

The new life we receive is a life of communion and friendship with the Father—obeying the Father just as Jesus did so that we can become "perfect, as your heavenly Father is perfect" (Matt 5:48). It's also life in Christ—being a part of his Body, the Church, and conforming our thoughts, words, and actions to the mind of Christ. Finally, this life means living as a temple of the Holy Spirit—holy and bearing spiritual fruit (CCC 1693–1695).

The Theological Virtues

At the foundation of the life of grace are faith, hope, and love. These are known as the three "theological virtues."

A virtue is defined as a "habitual and firm disposition to do the good" (CCC 1803). It's simpler, though, to just think of it as a good habit. It's something good we do or say or feel so often that eventually we don't even have to think about it; it just comes naturally. There are two different categories of virtues. First, there are "human virtues" or "moral virtues." These virtues help us live a morally good, more fully human life. We acquire the moral virtues primarily through our own effort—by working hard to consistently make good choices, which eventually form good habits that, in turn, make it easier for us to make good choices (CCC 1804).

The theological virtues are the second type of virtue. While the moral virtues help us live a more fully human life, the theological virtues help us live the divine life. They make us capable of loving God, acting as his children, and participating in his divine life. Both the source and the goal of these virtues is the same: God. He infuses them directly into our souls in Baptism to draw us into relationship with himself (CCC 1812–1813).

Faith

The first theological virtue is faith. Faith is the theological virtue by which we believe in God, in all that he has said and revealed to us, and in all that his Church proposes for our belief (CCC 1814). Faith, then, is the first requirement of a relationship with God. It's the beginning of our relationship with him and our life in Christ. Without it, we can't know or follow him. As the Council of Trent (1545–1563) says:

> "Faith is the beginning of human salvation," the foundation and root of all justification, "without which it is impossible to please God" (Heb. 11:6) and to come to the fellowship of His sons.[1]

---

[1] Council of Trent, Decree on Justification, in Henry Denzinger and Karl Rahner, eds. *The Sources of Catholic Dogma* (hereafter cited as DS), trans. Roy J. Deferrari (St. Louis,

Having faith means trusting in what God has revealed even when we don't always fully understand it. The teachings of the Church are sometimes difficult for us to grasp and require study, prayer, and conversion of heart to understand them correctly. For instance, we might find the Church's teaching on human sexuality hard to understand because it is so different from what is taught by today's culture, or we might resist it because it requires us to change our behavior. When we approach it in faith, though, studying the reasoning behind it, praying to God to give us understanding, and opening our hearts to be transformed by grace, it begins to make sense to us. Even then, though, our human minds simply aren't capable of grasping the fullness of some divine truths. Some of the things we believe in, like the Trinity, will always remain something of a mystery. We can grow in our understanding of the mystery, seeing it more deeply with time, prayer, study, and grace, but the fullness of that teaching still remains something that we can't fully comprehend this side of heaven.

To many people today, this seems like a weakness. Why would we put our faith in something we can't understand? Here, however, it's important to remember that faith isn't superstition or the abandonment of our intellect. Rather, it's is a *rational acknowledgement that God is essentially mysterious*—that, as Bishop Robert Barron says, "God is not one of the things in the world that I can see and know in the ordinary way."[2] It's an acceptance, based on evidence, that God exists, that he is trustworthy, and that there are going to be some truths that our human minds aren't capable of grasping simply because they are human; they have limits. Ultimately, this means that faith is not just subscribing to a list of beliefs but is, more fundamentally, a surrender to the hidden God—the God we can't see—and an act by which "man freely commits his entire self to God."[3]

MO: B. Herder Book Co., 1954), c. 8 (DS 1532), quoting St. Fulgentius, *De fide*, to Peter, note 1.

2 Bishop Robert Barron, "How Do We Know We Are Encountering God?" *Word on Fire*, August 2, 2007, https://www.wordonfire.org/resources/video/how-do-we-know-we-are-encountering-god/32/.

3 Second Vatican Council, Dogmatic Constitution on Divine Revelation *Dei Verbum* (November 18, 1965), §5.

Importantly, it is God himself who makes it possible for us to commit ourselves to him in this way. Faith, as a theological virtue, is a gift from God. At the same time, faith establishes a relationship with God that, like any relationship, needs care and attention to flourish. We allow God to deepen our faith when we open ourselves to him in prayer, in study, in the worship and sacraments of the Church, and when we remove sins, which are obstacles to our commitment to God, from our lives. We can also ask God to increase our faith. When we find ourselves struggling to believe, we can cry out, like the father of boy with the unclean spirit, "I believe; help my unbelief!" (Mark 9:24).

Hope

The second theological virtue, hope, is "the theological virtue by which we desire the kingdom of heaven and eternal life as our happiness, placing our trust in Christ's promises and relying not on our own strength, but on the help of the grace of the Holy Spirit" (CCC 1817).

In every human heart, God has placed a desire for happiness. This desire drives our actions; we do things and choose things that we think will make us happy. Because of original sin, however, our judgments on these matters aren't always correct. Often, what we think will make us happy makes us very unhappy. The theological virtue of hope, however, helps correct those judgments by orienting us toward true happiness. It takes our human desire for happiness and amplifies and directs it toward the kingdom of God. In short, it helps us to desire holiness and eternal life. It keeps our priorities straight, helping us to not lose sight of what matters most: heaven. It also helps us to trust in God and rely upon his help. This keeps us from being discouraged and inspires us to overcome selfishness and serve others with love (CCC 1818).

The Beatitudes give us a picture of the hope we have as disciples of Jesus (Matt 5:1–12). From a worldly perspective it can be hard to understand how the poor in spirit, the mourners, and the meek can be happy. When we understand how hope transforms our desires, though, their happiness makes sense. They're not looking to the things of the world for their happiness. Their desire isn't for power, money, prestige, pleasure, etc. Their desire is for God. Their desire is for the kingdom of heaven. That's what they know matters, and that's what they're seeking.

Hope can do the same for us. In times of sorrow and suffering, it reminds us that for those who love God, sorrow and suffering won't last. On occasions when we're tempted to break God's law in order to obtain some worldly good, it reminds us that God, not some fleeting pleasure, is what matters most. And if we ever find ourselves persecuted for what we believe, hope helps us hold fast to God, knowing that joy can only come from faithfulness to him.

We express this hope when we place our desires before God in prayer, trusting that he will provide for us even when things seem impossible (CCC 1820). In particular, the Our Father summarizes what the virtue of hope leads us to desire—that God's name will be glorified, that his kingdom will come, that his will shall be done, that he will provide for our needs, forgive our sins, and deliver us in our trials.

Love

The greatest of the theological virtues is love, which is also called charity. Charity is "the theological virtue by which we love God above all things for his own sake, and our neighbor as ourselves for the love of God" (CCC 1822).

Jesus makes it clear that love of God and love of others form the foundation upon which all the other commandments are based (Matt 22:37–40). If we truly love God and truly want to love others, we will fulfill all the requirements of the law and keep the commandments.

Perhaps the most famous description of love in Scripture comes from St. Paul's First Letter to the Corinthians, chapter 13. St. Paul tells us that no matter how great our gifts or how great our deeds, if we do not have love, we have nothing. All worldly things pass away, but the theological virtues—faith, hope, and love—remain, and the greatest of these is love.

Moreover, Jesus showed us what love truly is by loving his disciples "to the end" (John 13:1), laying down his life for us on the Cross. He tells us to follow this example of love, to love one another as he has loved us (John 15:12). This doesn't mean he wants each of us to literally give our life up for the sake of another. Some of us will indeed be called to make such a sacrifice. But all of us are called to love selflessly, not selfishly, putting the good of others before our own. We're all called to die to ourselves, choosing God's will over our will.

In friendship, this might mean listening to a friend talk about their day rather than complaining about our own problems. In romance, it means, in part, never asking your boyfriend or girlfriend to sin against chastity or do anything that might pull them away from God. In marriage, it might mean sacrificing a promotion at work that would take you away from your family or getting up in the middle of the night to care for a sick child rather than sleeping comfortably in bed. And it always means choosing God's will and obeying God's law—loving him by choosing his ways over our ways.

Our ability to show this kind of love is a grace. God gives it to us in order to strengthen and purify our human love and raise it to the supernatural perfection of divine love (CCC 1827). Jesus revealed God's love for us in dying on the Cross while we were still sinners. He also revealed that God *is* love—a Trinity of three Divine Persons united in love. Through Jesus, we receive and share in that love. Thus, love is at the center of our life in Christ on earth and what we hope for in heaven. It is the principle behind the commandments and virtues and the force that binds us in communion with God and the saints in eternity.

The Four Last Things

Death and Judgment

When our life is over, we will have to give an account to God for how we've responded to the grace he has offered us. When this day comes, Jesus will be our judge:

> Christ is Lord of eternal life. Full right to pass definitive judgment on the works and hearts of men belongs to him as redeemer of the world. He "acquired" this right by his cross. The

> Father has given "all judgment to the Son" [*Jn* 5:22; cf. *Jn* 5:27; *Mt* 25:31; *Acts* 10:42; 17:31; *2 Tim* 4:1]. Yet the Son did not come to judge, but to save and to give the life he has in himself [Cf. *Lk* 21:12; *Jn* 15:19–20]. By rejecting grace in this life, one already judges oneself, receives according to one's works, and can even condemn oneself for all eternity by rejecting the Spirit of love [Cf. *Jn* 3:18; 12:48; *Mt* 12:32; *1 Cor* 3:12–15; *Heb* 6:4–6; 10:26–31]. (CCC 679)

We won't, however, undergo just one judgment. We'll actually experience two. The first is called the Particular Judgment, and it will occur at the moment of our death. When we die, each of us will be judged according to our works and our acceptance or refusal of grace. In other words, did we love God and others? Did we work to overcome sin and vice? Did we serve and sacrifice for others? The answers to those questions will determine whether we will enter heaven immediately, enter hell immediately, or have to be purified in purgatory before entering heaven (CCC 1022).

The second judgment we will face is the General (or Last) Judgment. This will occur at the end of time when the dead rise from their graves and Christ returns in glory. At the Last Judgment, our souls will be reunited with our bodies, and the just will experience the resurrection of life—they will be like the risen Christ—but the unjust will go forth to the "resurrection of judgment" (John 5:28–29). The fate of each individual is determined at the Particular Judgment he or she experiences immediately after death, but at the Last Judgment, God will reveal all things. He will make known the full truth of our actions, our relationship with him, and his work of creation and salvation (CCC 1038–1041).

Death is the separation of the soul from the body. After death, the Church teaches, the body decays and the soul goes to meet God while it waits for the resurrection. At the Last Judgment, however, God will grant incorruptible life to our bodies by reuniting them with our souls. He will do this through the power of Jesus' Resurrection.

We confess our belief in this every Sunday when we recite the Creed, which culminates in our profession of faith in the resurrection of the dead and in life everlasting. This means that we believe and hope that just as Jesus rose from the dead and now lives forever, so too will we rise again when he returns in glory, and live forever in body and soul with him.

This hope developed gradually in Israel, as God revealed the truth of the resurrection to his people over time. In Jesus' time, the Pharisees and many other Jews believed in the resurrection of the dead. Jesus himself taught it, and he connected it to himself and his own Resurrection. Belief in the resurrection of the dead has been an essential element of the Christian faith from the beginning, but this belief has always faced opposition. While many people will accept that the soul lives on in some form after death, it seems incredible to some that our bodies, which are clearly mortal, could also share in everlasting life.

Christ's Resurrection, however, gives us some understanding of how the resurrection will occur. The bodies we are raised with will be our own bodies, but they will be glorified like his, and the life we return to will be different from this earthly life. The resurrection exceeds our imagination and understanding and is something that we can only know by faith, but St. Irenaeus explains that we receive a foretaste of it in the Eucharist:

> Just as bread that comes from the earth, after God's blessing has been invoked upon it, is no longer ordinary bread, but Eucharist, formed of two things, the one earthly and the other heavenly: so too our bodies, which partake of the Eucharist, are no longer corruptible, but possess the hope of resurrection.[4]

In a certain way, we have already risen with Jesus because Christian life on earth is already a participation in the death and Resurrection of Christ. United with Christ by Baptism and nourished by his Body in the Eucharist, believers already truly participate in the heavenly life of the risen Christ and belong to his Body, the Church (Col 2:12). Consequently, the body and soul of the believer belong to Christ in anticipation of the resurrection. As St. Paul says, "Do you not know that your bodies are members of Christ?" (1 Cor 6:15; CCC 1002–1004).

---

4 Irenaeus, *Against Heresies* 4.18.4–5, quoted in CCC 1000.

Heaven, Hell, and Purgatory

After the Particular Judgment at the moment of death, each soul proceeds either to heaven, hell, or purgatory (see Part IV, Chapter 4 of Course 2, Introduction to Christology). Together with death and judgment, heaven and hell are often described as "the four last things."

Heaven

Those who die in friendship with God and are perfectly purified live forever with Jesus in heaven. Heaven is a communion of life and love with the Holy Trinity, Mary, and all the saints and angels. It's the fulfillment of all our desires and the state of supreme happiness. There is, quite literally, nothing better than heaven. It's what all earthly happiness points to. It's the root of every longing and the fulfillment of why we were made. The greatest happiness we can feel on earth is just a hint of the happiness we will experience in heaven.

The souls in heaven enjoy this happiness in God's presence now. They don't have to wait for the Last Judgment to experience the joy of being close to God. But at the end of time, their bodies will rise from the dead and will also share in the glory of heaven like the risen Christ (CCC 1023–1024).

The communion with God and happiness of heaven are beyond what we can understand and describe and are only possible for us because God raises us up and shares his life with us through Christ. Nonetheless, the life of heaven is a continuation of the life in Christ in which we share even now through his Incarnation and Paschal Mystery. The friendship with God that we are meant to enjoy forever is something that he offers to us in Jesus Christ right here and right now. The closer we grow to him in this life, the more we choose his ways and spend time with him, the more our earth can become a foretaste of heaven (CCC 1025–1029).

Purgatory

Those who die in friendship with God but are not yet perfectly purified also go to heaven, but before they enter God's presence, their purification has to be completed in purgatory. This is where all the parts of us that are still selfish, still prideful, lustful, gluttonous, greedy, angry, envious, petty, and mean are, once and for all, rooted out of our souls. God wants us to fully enjoy all the happiness he has for us in heaven, and we can't do that when sin still has a claim on any part of us. The most loving thing God can do for us, when we're not fully ready for heaven, is get us ready. Traditionally this "getting ready" is described as a cleansing fire, but the fires of purgatory are completely different from the suffering of hell because purgatory isn't the end of their story (hence why it's not one of the four last things). The souls in purgatory know that they are preparing to enter the joy of heaven (CCC 1030–1031) and want nothing more than to have all the last traces of sin rooted out of their hearts so that they can be perfect for God.

Here on earth, we can help the souls in purgatory get what they desire through our prayers, almsgiving, indulgences, works of penance, and having Masses said on their behalf (CCC 1032). We also should remember that purgatory is the completion of the process of purification and sanctification that we begin in this life. While small sins (called "venial sins") don't break our relationship with God in a way that would deprive us of heaven, they do harm our relationship with him in a way that has to be repented of and healed either in this life or in purgatory. Thus, when we turn away from sins (even small ones), when we do penance and good works or obtain indulgences, and when we grow closer to God in holiness in this life, we bring the day that we will enter heaven closer. Importantly, it's always better to do this work now, while on earth, than wait to do it in purgatory. It's easier to do it here because we have bodies that can pray, sacrifice, go to Mass, and perform acts of penance. Here we can actively atone for our sins and ready our hearts for heaven, and then, when we do die, we don't have to wait to be with God. We get to be with him right away.

Hell

To be united with God in heaven, we have to freely choose to love him by keeping his commandments. When we sin gravely against him, against our neighbor, or against ourselves, we separate ourselves from him. If we die in mortal sin without repenting and accepting God's mercy, we will be separated from him forever by our own free choice. This separation from God is called hell (CCC 1033).

God doesn't predestine anyone to hell. He extends his mercy to everyone, and he calls everyone to repentance. But he also doesn't force us to love him. He gives us the freedom to reject him—even eternally. The warnings of Jesus and the teaching of the Church about hell show us how great a responsibility we have to use our freedom with our eternal destiny in mind: to choose the way that leads to life and avoid the path to destruction, to avoid and repent of grave sin, and to constantly seek out the mercy of God (CCC 1034–1037).

God's mercy always gives us hope. Hell is a terrible consequence of sin, but we must remember that God's mercy is greater than any sin we can commit. Even when we feel stuck in a habit of sin or when someone we love has turned away from God, we need to persevere in calling on God, never giving up hope, and knowing that Christ has won the ultimate victory over Satan and sin on the Cross.

SELECTED READING

Pope Benedict XVI, Encyclical Letter on Christian Hope *Spe Salvi* (November 30, 2007), nos. 41–44

At the conclusion of the central section of the Church's great *Credo*—the part that recounts the mystery of Christ, from his eternal birth of the Father and his temporal birth of the Virgin Mary, through his Cross and Resurrection to the second coming—we find the phrase: "he will come again in glory to judge the living and the dead." From the earliest times, the prospect of the Judgment has influenced Christians in their daily living as a criterion by which to order their present life, as a summons to their conscience, and at the same time as hope in God's justice. Faith in Christ has never looked merely backwards or merely upwards, but always also forwards to the hour of justice that the Lord repeatedly proclaimed. This looking ahead has given Christianity its importance for the present moment. In the arrangement of Christian sacred buildings, which were intended to make visible the historic and cosmic breadth of faith in Christ, it became customary to depict the Lord returning as a king—the symbol of hope—at the east end; while the west wall normally portrayed the Last Judgment as a symbol of our responsibility for our lives—a scene which followed and accompanied the faithful as they went out to resume their daily routine. As the iconography of the Last Judgment developed, however, more and more prominence was given to its ominous and frightening aspects, which obviously held more fascination for artists than the splendor of hope, often all too well concealed beneath the horrors.

In the modern era, the idea of the Last Judgment has faded into the background: Christian faith has been individualized and primarily oriented towards the salvation of the believer's own soul, while reflection on world history is largely dominated by the idea of progress. The fundamental content of awaiting a final Judgment, however, has not disappeared: it has simply taken on a totally different form. The atheism of the nineteenth and twentieth centuries is—in its origins and aims—a type of moralism: a protest against the injustices of the world and of world history. A world marked by so much injustice, innocent suffering, and cynicism of power cannot be the work of a good God. A God with responsibility for such a world would not be a just God, much less a good God. It is for the sake of morality that this God has to be contested. Since there is no God to create justice, it seems man himself is now called to establish justice. If, in the face of this world's suffering, protest against God is understandable, then the claim that humanity can and must do what no God actually does or is able to do is both presumptuous and intrinsically false. It is no accident that this idea has led to the greatest forms of cruelty and violations of justice. . . .

[In the face of all this, however, we must remember] God has given himself an "image": in Christ who was made man. In him who was crucified, the denial of false images of God is taken to an extreme. God now reveals his true face in the figure of the sufferer who shares man's God-forsaken condition by taking it upon himself. This innocent sufferer has attained the certitude of hope: there is a God, and

God can create justice in a way that we cannot conceive, yet we can begin to grasp it through faith. Yes, there is a resurrection of the flesh. There is justice. There is an "undoing" of past suffering, a reparation that sets things aright. For this reason, faith in the Last Judgement is first and foremost hope—the need for which was made abundantly clear in the upheavals of recent centuries. I am convinced that the question of justice constitutes the essential argument, or in any case the strongest argument, in favour of faith in eternal life. The purely individual need for a fulfillment that is denied to us in this life, for an everlasting love that we await, is certainly an important motive for believing that man was made for eternity; but only in connection with the impossibility that the injustice of history should be the final word does the necessity for Christ's return and for new life become fully convincing.

To protest against God in the name of justice is not helpful. A world without God is a world without hope (cf. *Eph* 2:12). Only God can create justice. And faith gives us the certainty that he does so. The image of the Last Judgment is not primarily an image of terror, but an image of hope; for us it may even be the decisive image of hope. Is it not also a frightening image? I would say: it is an image that evokes responsibility, an image, therefore, of that fear of which Saint Hilary spoke when he said that all our fear has its place in love. God is justice and creates justice. This is our consolation and our hope. And in his justice there is also grace. This we know by turning our gaze to the crucified and risen Christ. Both these things—justice and grace—must be seen in their correct inner relationship. Grace does not cancel out justice. It does not make wrong into right. It is not a sponge which wipes everything away, so that whatever someone has done on earth ends up being of equal value. Dostoevsky, for example, was right to protest against this kind of Heaven and this kind of grace in his novel *The Brothers Karamazov*. Evildoers, in the end, do not sit at table at the eternal banquet beside their victims without distinction, as though nothing had happened. Here I would like to quote a passage from Plato which expresses a premonition of just judgment that in many respects remains true and salutary for

Christians too. Albeit using mythological images, he expresses the truth with an unambiguous clarity, saying that in the end souls will stand naked before the judge. It no longer matters what they once were in history, but only what they are in truth: "Often, when it is the king or some other monarch or potentate that he (the judge) has to deal with, he finds that there is no soundness in the soul whatever; he finds it scourged and scarred by the various acts of perjury and wrong-doing . . . ; it is twisted and warped by lies and vanity, and nothing is straight because truth has had no part in its development. Power, luxury, pride, and debauchery have left it so full of disproportion and ugliness that when he has inspected it (he) sends it straight to prison, where on its arrival it will undergo the appropriate punishment. . . . Sometimes, though, the eye of the judge lights on a different soul which has lived in purity and truth . . . then he is struck with admiration and sends him to the isles of the blessed."

QUESTIONS FOR REVIEW

1. Can we earn our own salvation and a place in heaven?
2. What are the three theological virtues? Give a short definition of each.
3. What is the Particular Judgment?
4. What is the Last Judgment?
5. What are the four last things? Give a short description of each.

QUESTIONS FOR DISCUSSION

1. For each of the theological virtues, give one example of what that virtue looks like in action in your own life. In other words, give one concrete example of how you have demonstrated faith, hope, and charity.

2. Knowing that one day you will see Jesus face to face and he will judge all your actions, what is one thing you have done that you are proud of? What is one thing you would want to do differently going forward?
3. The Church encourages us to think often about the four last things. Why do think she does this?

Chapter 2

We Are Called to Holiness

All Christians are called to holiness—to be conformed to Christ and to share in the life of the Holy Trinity. Our task is nothing short of the call issued by Jesus in the Gospel of Matthew: "be perfect, as your heavenly Father is perfect" (Matt 5:48).

When we hear the word holiness, we might think about someone who is so good they don't seem real or someone who acts like they're better than everybody else. We might even think about someone who is boring and no fun to be around. But that's not what holiness is at all! A holy person is someone who is filled with love and joy. They aren't weighed down by the sadness of sin, and so they're free to truly be the person God made them to be. Holy people are deeply and truly human people. They are the ones who are really and truly themselves, and that makes them a blessing to be around . . . and even fun to be around!

A lot of times, we also can trick ourselves into thinking that this call to holiness is just for priests or monks and nuns or the saints of the past. But that's not the case. It's for every single person who has been baptized. Through Baptism, God cleanses us from sin and makes us holy. Baptism makes us like Christ. It makes us adopted sons and daughters of God. But Baptism is just the beginning. It removes original sin and any personal sins we may have committed, but it doesn't take away our tendency to sin (concupiscence). Consequently, the Christian life remains a struggle and a journey. We have to continually strive to live up to the gift we have received in Baptism (CCC 2012–2013, 2813).

As we strive to do that, we become more closely united to Jesus. This union is called a "mystical" union. This doesn't necessarily mean that we will receive extraordinary mystical signs like the visions or miracles experienced by some saints, but it does mean that as Christians we will share in the mysteries of Christ's incarnation and life (especially in the "sacred mysteries" of the sacraments) and, through Christ, in the mystery of the Holy Trinity (CCC 2014).

Ultimately, at the heart of holiness is love, or charity, the greatest of the theological virtues. Holiness leads us to follow the commandments, which tell us to love God above all things and love our neighbor as ourselves. Charity also leads us to imitate Jesus, who gave his life out of love for us. It unites us to the Holy Trinity, which is a communion of love, and it unites us in love with our fellow Christians in the Church (CCC 826). The Church is united by love and fulfills its mission when its members live in love and holiness. In other words, when we grow in holiness in the Church, we help build up the Church (CCC 2045).

God's Call and Our Response

One of the first and most fundamental truths we learn from Scripture is that God has made us in his own image (Gen 1:26–27). Just as children are made in their parents' image, we are made in God's image. Like him, we possess the ability to love, reason, and choose right from wrong. We have an immortal soul, a soul that was made to live forever. We have the power of reason so that we can understand the world around us, and we have free will so that we can direct our actions in the right direction, toward goodness. All these gifts, which come from God and are reflections of him, direct us to what is true and good. Using them well is how we become more like Jesus. They help us find our ultimate fulfillment, what truly satisfies us and truly brings us joy: God himself (CCC 1703–1705).

Reason and free will are tremendous gifts. They come, however, with equally tremendous responsibilities. Unlike animals, we aren't driven solely by instinct, so we have to choose to respond to God's call to holiness. Likewise, reason allows us to recognize the voice of God in our conscience, which tells us that we must do what is good and avoid what is evil, but we must freely choose to follow this law ourselves—we must respond to God's call by the way we live our lives (CCC 1706, 2002).

We respond to God's call and grow in holiness through the choices we make. We have to follow our conscience in choosing what is right in the small day-to-day matters—like helping out at home, not cheating on tests, and being kind to others—and in the larger decisions of our life that determine our vocation—not committing sexual sin, faithfully praying and going to Mass, and listening to God's prompts to study certain things or serve in a certain way. The call to holiness that each Christian receives takes the shape of a particular vocation—a particular way of life, such as religious life or marriage—and how well we listen to God and follow his will for us throughout our life shapes our ability to pursue the vocation he has for us.

This call of God's—both in small matters and big matters—does occasionally come through an audible voice. Much, much more often, though, God simply speaks to us through our conscience. Many people in our culture misuse this term. They equate it with a feeling or an emotion. The Catechism, however, defines it differently, stating that

> Conscience is a judgment of reason whereby the human person recognizes the moral quality of a concrete act that he is going to perform, is in the process of performing, or has already completed. In all he says and does, man is obliged to follow faithfully what he knows to be just and right. (CCC 1778)

This means that conscience isn't primarily a kind of direct inspiration of God or even a matter of what we "feel" is right, but rather is a matter of recognizing with our God-given reason whether an action that we are considering is right or wrong.

Silence, reflection, and sincere listening are crucial for developing our conscience and hearing its voice. Daily prayer and reflection on the lives and writings of the saints and other good and holy people can also help us hear the "still, small voice" of God speaking to us through our conscience (1 Kgs 19:12). We should likewise make a daily habit of examining our lives to see how we have acted, how other people reacted to our actions, what we feel good about, and what, perhaps, we think we could have done differently. Through this careful reflection, practiced as a consistent part of daily prayer, God's will for our lives will be revealed to us and he will give us the grace we need to follow his will and grow in holiness. As Jesus said, "Ask, and it will be given you" (Matt 7:7).

Holiness Is God's Gift

Following our conscience and growing in holiness are not always easy, but God gives us the grace to respond to his call. Through Christ's victory over sin on the Cross, God offers us strength when we are tempted, and forgiveness and healing when we fail. When we persevere in our vocation, relying on him for strength and forgiveness, we grow in holiness and union with him.

God's grace comes to us especially in the Church and the sacraments. Through the grace of Baptism, which makes us part of the Body of Christ, and the gifts of the Holy Spirit conferred at Confirmation, we receive strength and help to live a life of holiness. Through Penance, we receive forgiveness and grace to change our lives when we fail. Through the sacraments of Matrimony and Holy Orders, those who are called to marriage or the priesthood receive the grace needed to live out their vocations. And through the Eucharist, we receive the spiritual nourishment and communion with Jesus and our fellow believers that sustains us.

God also helps us to grow in holiness through the teaching and guidance of our pope, bishops, and priests, through the support of our fellow believers, and through the example and prayers of the saints. In our struggle to hear and answer God's call, we are never alone. Joined together with our fellow believers, we receive strength from their love, encouragement, prayers, and good example. In turn, through our love, encouragement, prayers, and good example, we strengthen others. The more this mutual strengthening unfolds, the more the Body of Christ truly reflects the holiness of Christ, who is the Head of the Body (CCC 2045).

SELECTED READING

Second Vatican Council, Dogmatic Constitution on the Church *Lumen Gentium* (November 21, 1964), nos. 40–41

The Lord Jesus, the divine Teacher and Model of all perfection, preached holiness of life to each and every one of His disciples of every condition. He Himself stands as the author and consumator of this holiness of life: "Be you therefore perfect, even as your heavenly Father is perfect." Indeed He sent the Holy Spirit upon all men that He might move them inwardly to love God with their whole heart and their whole soul, with all their mind and all their strength and that they might love each other as Christ loves them. The followers of Christ are called by God, not because of their works, but according to His own purpose and grace. They are justified in the Lord Jesus, because in the baptism of faith they truly become sons of God and sharers in the divine nature. In this way they are really made holy. Then too, by God's gift, they must hold on to and complete in their lives this holiness they have received. They are warned by the Apostle to live "as becomes saints," and to put on "as God's chosen ones, holy and beloved a heart of mercy, kindness, humility, meekness, patience," and to possess the fruit of the Spirit in holiness. Since truly we all offend in many things we all need God's mercies continually and we all must daily pray: "Forgive us our debts."

Thus it is evident to everyone, that all the faithful of Christ of whatever rank or status, are called to the fullness of the Christian life and to the perfection of charity; by this holiness as such a more human manner of living is promoted in this earthly society. In order that the faithful may reach this perfection, they must use their strength accordingly as they have received it, as a gift from Christ. They must follow in His footsteps and conform themselves to His image seeking the will of the Father in all things. They must devote themselves with all their being to the glory of God and the service of their neighbor. In this way, the holiness of the People of God will grow into an abundant harvest of good, as is admirably shown by the life of so many saints in Church history.

The classes and duties of life are many, but holiness is one—that sanctity which is cultivated by all who are moved by the Spirit of God, and who obey the voice of the Father and worship God the Father in spirit and in truth. These people follow the poor Christ, the humble and cross-bearing Christ in order to be worthy of being sharers in His glory. Every person must walk unhesitatingly according to his own personal gifts and duties in the path of living faith, which arouses hope and works through charity.

In the first place, the shepherds of Christ's flock must holily and eagerly, humbly and courageously carry out their ministry, in imitation of the eternal high Priest, the Shepherd and Guardian of our souls. They ought to fulfill this duty in such a way that it will be the principal means also of their own sanctification. . . .

Priests, who resemble bishops to a certain degree in their participation of the sacrament of Orders, form the spiritual crown of the bishops. They participate in the grace of their office and they should grow daily in their love of God and their neighbor by the exercise of their office through Christ, the eternal and unique Mediator. They should preserve the bond of priestly communion, and they should abound in every spiritual good and thus present to all men a living witness to God. . . .

Furthermore, married couples and Christian parents should follow their own proper path (to holiness) by faithful love. They should sustain one another in grace throughout the entire length of their lives. They should embue their offspring, lovingly welcomed as God's gift, with Christian doctrine and the evangelical virtues. In this manner, they offer all men the example of unwearying and generous love; in this way they build up the brotherhood of charity; in so doing, they stand as the witnesses and cooperators in the fruitfulness of Holy Mother Church; by such lives, they are a sign and

> a participation in that very love, with which Christ loved His Bride and for which He delivered Himself up for her. A like example, but one given in a different way, is that offered by widows and single people, who are able to make great contributions toward holiness and apostolic endeavor in the Church. Finally, those who engage in labor—and frequently it is of a heavy nature—should better themselves by their human labors. They should be of aid to their fellow citizens. They should raise all of society, and even creation itself, to a better mode of existence. Indeed, they should imitate by their lively charity, in their joyous hope and by their voluntary sharing of each others' burdens, the very Christ who plied His hands with carpenter's tools and Who in union with His Father, is continually working for the salvation of all men. In this, then, their daily work they should climb to the heights of holiness and apostolic activity.

QUESTIONS FOR REVIEW

1. Who is called to holiness?
2. What virtue is at the heart of holiness?
3. What is our conscience?
4. How does our conscience help us in the pursuit of holiness?
5. How do the different sacraments help us in the pursuit of holiness?

QUESTIONS FOR DISCUSSION

1. When you think of holiness, what's the first thing that comes to mind? Why do you think this is?
2. Do you want to be holy? Why or why not?
3. What do you think a "holy" you would be like? How would you be the same as you are today? How would you be different?

Chapter 3

Living as a Disciple of Jesus

Jesus himself is the way to holiness and salvation. We respond to God's call by living as his disciples.

In the Introduction to Christology, we learned about what it means to be a disciple of Jesus. Jesus, remember, is the Messiah. Fully God and fully man, he came to earth and emptied himself out of love for us. Accordingly, to be his disciple requires more than just learning from his teachings; it requires loving him as Savior. He is the perfect revelation of God, who is truth itself, so we need to serve him as Lord and reverently accept his teachings. He is also the "perfect man"—the perfect revelation of what it means to be human—so we need to follow his example and seek to become like him in everything we do (CCC 520, 562).

The truth that Jesus reveals about God and the example that he gives as a man are summed up in the Paschal Mystery of his suffering, death, and Resurrection. The Paschal Mystery reveals the depths of God's love for us. Indeed, Jesus revealed that God *is* love (1 John 4:8). Jesus, the Son of God, came to us as a man, "not to be served but to serve, and to give his life as a ransom for many" (Matt 20:28). The example he gave us to follow was one of poverty and humility, accepting the sufferings and persecutions that came his way and obeying the Father even to the point of the humiliating death on the Cross.

We, in turn, as the recipients of such great gifts, are called to empty ourselves, both in love for others and in obedience to God as he did. By taking up our own cross and following him, we act as partners in the Paschal Mystery, which redeems us. We become conformed to him, and through him we share in communion with the Father (CCC 618).

Conversion

Our life as followers of Jesus begins where Jesus' preaching began: with the call to conversion. "Repent, and believe in the gospel," he cried out, over and over again (Mark 1:15). This call asks us to do more than just admit fault for our sins; it asks us to dramatically change our lives and turn to God. The Catechism explains:

> Interior repentance is a radical reorientation of our whole life, a return, a conversion to God with all our heart, an end of sin, a turning away from evil, with repugnance toward the evil actions we have committed. At the same time it entails the desire and resolution to change one's life, with hope in God's mercy and trust in the help of his grace. (CCC 1431)

The call to conversion is addressed, in part, to those who don't know Jesus and his Gospel. For them, conversion begins with Baptism: "It is by faith in the Gospel and by Baptism [Cf. *Acts* 2:38] that one renounces evil and gains salvation, that is, the forgiveness of all sins and the gift of new life" (CCC 1427).

But the call to conversion isn't just addressed to the unbaptized. It's addressed to all of us: to those of us who are baptized but don't take our faith seriously; to those of us who've grown up in the faith but don't live our lives like we truly believe; to those of us who receive the sacraments regularly but are also trapped in patterns of sin; and to those of us who've walked away from the faith, whether in fact or just in our hearts. Some people answer this call slowly, as life unfolds and their faith deepens. Some answer it in a dramatic fashion, radically changing their lives in response to the Gospel's call. And some people never answer it at all.

However we first hear the call, when we begin to follow Jesus, we soon realize that the need for conversion continues throughout our lives. It's not a once and done kind of thing. Whenever we look to Jesus as our example and compare his life to our own, we see our need for ongoing conversion. In fact, the closer we grow to Jesus, the more clearly we understand the implications of his example and teaching and the more clearly we know our own faults.

The process of ongoing conversion is driven, in part, by the formation of our conscience. As we learned in Chapter 2, conscience is a judgment of reason about the moral rightness or wrongness of our actions. Our reason, however, can be distorted by sin or ignorance, so our conscience has to be educated. This is clear in the case of small children, who often can't recognize how their actions affect other people and have to be carefully taught by their parents. But this process of maturing and growing shouldn't end as we grow up. It should continue throughout our lives. This is what makes it so important to study the Church's teachings, read the lives of the saints, attend retreats, and listen to talks about the faith, as well as persist in prayer and worship. As Catholics, we have a rich treasury of wisdom to draw upon that will help us form our consciences in accord with the truth and learn better how to love and serve others.

Loving God and Neighbor

The Letter of St. James teaches clearly that, to be followers of Jesus, it is not enough to just listen to his teachings. We have to put them into practice:

> But be doers of the word, and not hearers only, deceiving yourselves. For if any one is a hearer of the word and not a doer, he is like a man who observes his natural face in a mirror; for he observes himself and goes away and at once forgets what he was like. But he who looks into the perfect law, the law of liberty, and perseveres, being no hearer that forgets but a doer that acts, he shall be blessed in his doing. (James 1:22–25)

Jesus' moral and spiritual teachings are centered on love. He summarizes all the commandments with the two greatest commandments: to love God with all our strength and to love our neighbor as ourselves. Thus, love is at the center of discipleship, and we put Jesus' teachings into practice by worshipping and loving God and loving our neighbors as Jesus has taught us.

Worshipping God is central to the life of a disciple. If you don't worship God, then you're not following Jesus. Remember, when Jesus is asked what the greatest commandment is, he quotes the Book of Deuteronomy: "Hear, O Israel: The Lord our God, the Lord is one; and you shall love the Lord your God with all your heart, and with all your soul, and with all your mind, and with all your strength" (Mark 12:29–30; see Deut 6:4–5).

As our almighty Creator, God deserves the love and worship of his creatures as a matter of justice—just as parents deserve to be loved and respected by their children. But throughout this course, we have seen how much God has loved us first. He created us out of love to share in his life, and even when we turned from him in sin, he sought us out in love and brought us back to him. Finally, he sent his Son, Jesus, who shared our life and gave himself up to death out of love for us. God loves us so much that the response of a loving heart is to love him back, giving him our own love and worship as Jesus taught us, through a life centered on the sacraments and prayer.

Jesus, the Book of Hebrews tells us, is our great high priest. His Paschal Mystery is the perfect act of worship, which fulfilled the worship of the Old Testament and restored us to union with God. He is the one mediator between God and man, and the Head of the Church, so we have communion with God through him as a part of his Body, the Church. Likewise, we are united to the Church and share in his Paschal Mystery through the sacraments, which he gave the Church as a means of grace.

Thus, loving and worshipping God as Jesus taught means living a sacramental life. Baptism establishes this life in us by giving us sanctifying grace and the theological virtues. Confirmation strengthens our bond to Christ and his Church, so that we can fulfill the call to holiness. Penance restores the grace of our Baptism when we lose it through sin, and the Anointing of the Sick gives us strength and courage when we are seriously ill. Matrimony and Holy Orders consecrate those called to marriage or the priesthood for the service of the Church.

Above all, though, a sacramental life is centered on the Holy Eucharist. The Second Vatican Council calls the Mass "the source and summit of the Christian life."[1] The other sacraments and the whole life of the Church point to the Eucharist, because the Eucharist unites us to Christ and his Paschal Mystery. In the Mass, we participate, with the rest of the Church, in Christ's perfect act of worship, uniting our lives with his offering of himself on the Cross (see Part IV, Chapter 2). We are required to participate in Mass every Sunday and on holy days of obligation because "it is right and just" to give God the thanks and praise we owe him and because the Eucharist is our "daily bread"—the spiritual nourishment we need to sustain our spiritual life and our relationship with Christ.[2]

Our relationship with God must also be nourished by prayer. Like our human relationships, our relationship with God requires communication and conversation. God has spoken to us in divine Revelation, transmitted through Scripture and Sacred Tradition, and we speak back to him when we pray. In prayer, our faith, hope, and love come alive. We thank him, we praise him, and we ask him to provide for our needs and the needs of others, believing and trusting that he can and will care for us.

When it comes to how to pray, we have the best teacher: Jesus himself. He is our model for prayer, and because he himself intercedes for us eternally with the Father, our prayers become effective through him (John 15:16). He also tells us to be persistent and constant in prayer (Luke 18:1). This means we need to form a habit of prayer, calling on God in all our needs and raising our minds to him throughout the day—when we wake up, before we go to school, as we study, compete, and even as we hang out with our friends—so that prayer pervades our entire lives, making every day an act of worship.

---

1 Second Vatican Council, Dogmatic Constitution on the Church *Lumen Gentium* (November 21, 1964), 11.

2 Order of Mass, 31; Matt 6:11.

The Evangelical Counsels

> ASSIGNED READING
> Luke 10:29–37

Some Christians are called to dedicate their lives to God in a particular way through what are called the "evangelical counsels" of poverty, chastity, and obedience. Monks, nuns, religious brothers and sisters, and others who live a form of consecrated life make vows to not own their own property (poverty), to not marry but remain celibate (chastity), and to obey the superiors of their community (obedience). These counsels enable them to dedicate themselves more perfectly to prayer and the service of others. Not everyone is called to live out the evangelical counsels in this way, but there are aspects of poverty, chastity, and obedience that must be lived out in every way of life.

We must, for instance, not be obsessed with money and possessions, but share freely of what God has given us. We must live out the virtue of chastity according to our state in life. We must obey those who exercise just authority over us: parents, teachers, civil authorities, and bishops and priests in the Church, and through it all, we must love our neighbor (CCC 915, 1986). In this, like in all things, Jesus is our model.

Loving as Jesus Loved

> God shows his love for us in that while we were yet sinners Christ died for us. (Rom 5:8)

When Jesus reveals the command to love our neighbors as ourselves, a lawyer asks, "And who is my neighbor?" (Luke 10:29). Jesus answers the question with the Parable of the Good Samaritan, which shows us that our love can't be limited to just our close friends and family. It must extend to everyone in need of compassion, especially those who are ignored or cast aside by society—the poor, the elderly, the sick, the unborn, the marginalized, those with special needs, and those who struggle with particular sins. Jesus himself gives us an example of this in that, while we were still far from God because of our sins, he came and died to save us.

> Love your enemies and pray for those who persecute you. (Matt 5:44)

Jesus also shows us that our love must extend even to our enemies. When he is arrested, he doesn't defend himself, and he tells Peter to put away his sword (Matt 26:52). Then, from the Cross, he prays for his persecutors: "Father, forgive them; for they know not what they do" (Luke 23:34). He asks us to do the same. We are to renounce wrath, hatred, and vengeance and show love to those who wish to harm us (Matt 5:22–39; CCC 2262).

> Greater love has no man than this, that a man lay down his life for his friends. (John 15:13)

Loving as Jesus loves ultimately means laying down our lives just as he did. We may not need to literally suffer death for others, but we all must see our lives and everything we have as a gift from God, which we are meant to give freely in return. God is the source of our life, our talents, our possessions, and all of creation. Everything good that we have—our bodies, our family and friends, the air we breathe—comes from him, and we are stewards, not masters, of these gifts. Like the servants in the Parable of the Talents (Matt 25:14–30), we must not squander these gifts or hold them tightly to ourselves, but care for them and put them to use serving others and building up his kingdom. Like Jesus, love means emptying ourselves, pouring out every blessing we possess to bless others in turn (Phil 2:6–7; CCC 1823).

> Go therefore and make disciples of all nations, baptizing them in the name of the Father and of the Son and of the Holy Spirit, teaching them to observe all that I have commanded you. (Matt 28:19–20)

One of the best gifts we've been given as followers of Jesus is the good news of salvation. Like the other gifts we've received, it is not meant to be kept to ourselves but is meant to be shared. After all, loving our neighbors means not just looking after their physical good, but their spiritual good as well. We can't do that if we're not willing to tell them about the God who loves them and wants a relationship with them.

Speaking up about Jesus and sharing our faith can be difficult. It can feel awkward and even scary when we don't know how people will react or what they will think of us. But, the closer we grow to Jesus and the longer we follow him as a disciple, the easier it gets. It starts to feel natural, and eventually it actually feels much harder to not talk about Jesus and all he has done for us. It also helps that the more closely we follow Jesus, the more like him we become, and so, in time, our lives themselves are able to show people, in part, who Jesus is and what it means to follow him.

SELECTED READING

Pope Benedict XVI, Encyclical Letter on Christian Hope *Spe Salvi* (November 30, 2007), nos. 28–29

Our relationship with God is established through communion with Jesus—we cannot achieve it alone or from our own resources alone. The relationship with Jesus, however, is a relationship with the one who gave himself as a ransom for all (cf. *1 Tim* 2:6). Being in communion with Jesus Christ draws us into his "being for all"; it makes it our own way of being. He commits us to live for others, but only through communion with him does it become possible truly to be there for others, for the whole. In this regard I would like to quote the great Greek Doctor of the Church, Maximus the Confessor († 662), who begins by exhorting us to prefer nothing to the knowledge and love of God, but then quickly moves on to practicalities: "The one who loves God cannot hold on to money but rather gives it out in God's fashion . . . in the same manner in accordance with the measure of justice." Love of God leads to participation in the justice and generosity of God towards others. Loving God requires an interior freedom from all possessions and all material goods: the love of God is revealed in responsibility for others. This same connection between love of God and responsibility for others can be seen in a striking way in the life of Saint Augustine. After his conversion to the Christian faith, he decided, together with some like-minded friends, to lead a life totally dedicated to the word of God and to things eternal. His intention was to practice a Christian version of the ideal of the contemplative life expressed in the great tradition of Greek philosophy, choosing in this way the "better part" (cf. *Lk* 10:42). Things turned out differently, however. While attending the Sunday liturgy at the port city of Hippo, he was called out from the assembly by the Bishop and constrained to receive ordination for the exercise of the priestly ministry in that city. Looking back on that moment, he writes in his Confessions: "Terrified by my sins and the weight of my misery, I had resolved in my heart, and meditated flight into the wilderness; but you forbade me and gave me strength, by saying: 'Christ died for all, that those who live might live no longer for themselves but for him who for their sake died' (cf. 2 *Cor* 5:15)." Christ died for all. To live for him means allowing oneself to be drawn into his being for others.

For Augustine this meant a totally new life. He once described his daily life in the following terms: "The turbulent have to be corrected, the faint-hearted cheered up, the weak supported; the Gospel's opponents need to be refuted, its insidious enemies guarded against; the unlearned need to be taught, the indolent stirred up, the argumentative checked; the proud must be put in their place, the desperate set on their feet, those engaged in quarrels reconciled; the needy have to be helped, the oppressed to be liberated, the good to be encouraged, the bad to be tolerated; all must be loved." "The Gospel terrifies me"—producing that healthy fear which prevents us from living for ourselves alone and compels us to pass on the hope we hold in common. Amid the serious difficulties facing the Roman Empire—and also posing a serious threat to Roman Africa, which was actually destroyed at the end of Augustine's life—this was what he set out to do: to transmit hope, the hope which came to him from

> faith and which, in complete contrast with his introverted temperament, enabled him to take part decisively and with all his strength in the task of building up the city. In the same chapter of the *Confessions* in which we have just noted the decisive reason for his commitment "for all," he says that Christ "intercedes for us, otherwise I should despair. My weaknesses are many and grave, many and grave indeed, but more abundant still is your medicine. We might have thought that your word was far distant from union with man, and so we might have despaired of ourselves, if this Word had not become flesh and dwelt among us." On the strength of his hope, Augustine dedicated himself completely to the ordinary people and to his city—renouncing his spiritual nobility, he preached and acted in a simple way for simple people.

QUESTIONS FOR REVIEW

1. To whom is the call to conversion addressed?
2. What does "ongoing conversion" mean?
3. What are three things that can help us in the process of ongoing conversion?
4. What are the evangelical counsels?
5. What are two ways of loving our neighbor modeled for us by Jesus?

QUESTIONS FOR DISCUSSION

1. What is one practical thing you could do to show your love for God more?
2. What is one practical thing you could do to show your love for your family more?
3. Are you comfortable sharing your faith with others? Why or why not? What is one practical thing you could do to help others know about God's love?

Part VI

Prayer in the Life of a Believer

We've already mentioned the importance of prayer several times in this course. This is because a life of love for God and our neighbor is only possible if it's anchored in a living, personal relationship with God that is nourished by prayer. Developing a rich life of prayer, however, can be a real challenge and raises many questions for most of us, questions like: How do we approach God in prayer? Should our prayer be formal, like in Church, or should it to be like talking to a friend? And what do we do when it seems like our prayers aren't being answered?

These questions can be difficult, not only for a beginner but also for the most experienced contemplative monks and nuns. So, in Part IV, we're going to try to provide some answers.

Chapter 1

God Calls Every Individual to Prayer

It's easy to tell ourselves that a rich prayer life is only for a select minority of Christians—for priests and nuns and saintly grandparents, but not for young people or the average (and busy!) lay Catholic. But this is just an excuse. In the depths of our heart, we know that God calls each of us to share ourselves with him in prayer. As St. Augustine says: "You have made us for yourself, O Lord, and our hearts are restless until they rest in you."[1]

God calls every one of us to a close, personal, intimate relationship with him, and the natural response of the human heart to this call is prayer. The Catechism explains:

> Where does prayer come from? Whether prayer is expressed in words or gestures, it is the whole man who prays. But in naming the source of prayer, Scripture speaks sometimes of the soul or the spirit, but most often of the heart (more than a thousand times). According to Scripture, it is the *heart* that prays. If our

---

1 Augustine of Hippo, "The Confessions of St. Augustine," in *The Confessions and Letters of St. Augustin, with a Sketch of His Life and Work*, ed. Philip Schaff, trans. J. G. Pilkington, vol. 1, A Select Library of the Nicene and Post-Nicene Fathers of the Christian Church, First Series (Buffalo, NY: Christian Literature Company, 1886), 1.1.

heart is far from God, the words of prayer are in vain. (CCC 2562)

So, what form does this response, this prayer from the heart, take?

What Is Prayer?

St. John of Damascus famously described prayer as "the raising of one's mind and heart to God or the requesting of good things from God."[2] This simple yet profound definition is a starting point for understanding what prayer is. Perhaps another way of putting it is that we "offer" our mind and heart to God. When we join in any conversation, we offer someone our mind. We add to the conversation by speaking aloud our thoughts. We adjust our words according to the flow of the conversation. As the frequency of our conversations grow and we become friends, we may begin to offer our hearts, sharing our most intimate thoughts and deepest feelings. With close friends and family, the tone of our conversations are deeper because we have developed love.

The process of prayer really is a kind of "falling in love" because we are drawn into conversation and relationship with God. Prayer, therefore, is a necessary part of fulfilling the first and the greatest commandment, "You shall love the Lord your God with all your heart, and with all your soul, and with all your mind" (Matt 22:37). We owe our love and worship to God as a matter of justice, but loving God isn't only a matter of keeping the commandments and sharing in the Church's liturgical worship. Love requires conversation. It requires the offering up of the mind and heart. We can never "repay" God for creating us and saving us through Jesus, but our love and gratitude should show itself by answering the call he has placed in our hearts—to spend time with him and develop a real relationship of love in prayer.

---

[2] John Damascene, "An Exact Exposition of the Orthodox Faith," in *St. Hilary of Poitiers, John of Damascus*, ed. Philip Schaff and Henry Wace, trans. S. D. F. Salmond, vol. 9, A Select Library of the Nicene and Post-Nicene Fathers of the Christian Church, Second Series (New York: Christian Literature Company, 1899), 3.24.

Prayer as Communion with Jesus

As we've already mentioned, when we say that prayer is like a conversation, this doesn't necessarily mean that God will respond to our prayers with an audible voice. While it does sometimes happen that God reveals himself in a special way to particular people through private revelations or spiritual experiences, most people don't ordinarily receive these kinds of graces. This doesn't mean, however, that God doesn't speak to us. Prayer makes us attentive to how God can speak to us and how he can be present to us through our ordinary experiences—in the blessings he gives us (or doesn't give us), in the movements of our heart, or in the words of the people he puts in our lives.

But however we may hear God speaking to us privately, conversation with God requires listening first of all to how he has spoken publicly in divine Revelation, handed down to us in Scripture and Tradition. To hear God in prayer, we need to listen to his word in Scripture and Tradition, and—most important—we need to listen to the one that Scripture and Tradition reveals: his Son, Jesus Christ.

Jesus is the Word of God and the mediator between God and man, who intercedes for us at the right hand of the Father. Through him, God speaks to us, and through him, we have access to the Father. Even though God is infinite and all-powerful, and even though we had separated ourselves from him by sin, we're able to have a relationship with him because he has sent us his Son, Jesus, to reconcile us to him (see Part II, Chapter 3). Jesus is united to us through his human nature, so we can relate to him as a human being. As a human being, Jesus himself prayed, and because he is the Son of God, perfectly obedient to the Father's will, his prayers are always effective: "In the days of his flesh, Jesus offered up prayers and supplications, with loud cries and tears, to him who was able to save him from death, and he was heard for his godly fear" (Heb 5:7). Because of Jesus, our prayers—when they are united to him—are effective as well: "Whatever you ask in my name, I will do it, that the Father may be glorified in the Son; if you ask anything in my name, I will do it" (John 14:13–14).

Prayer puts us in relationship with all three Persons of the Trinity: The prayer of the Church is addressed above all to the Father (CCC

2665), and it is the Holy Spirit who moves us to prayer (CCC 2670). But Jesus is the one mediator between God and man, so developing a relationship with God in prayer means getting to know Jesus:

> There is no other way of Christian prayer than Christ. Whether our prayer is communal or personal, vocal or interior, it has access to the Father only if we pray "in the name" of Jesus. The sacred humanity of Jesus is therefore the way by which the Holy Spirit teaches us to pray to God our Father. (CCC 2664)

While he lived on earth, Jesus' disciples interacted with him face-to-face, like any human being, but before he ascended to heaven, he promised to remain with his disciples to the end of the age (Matt 28:20). This presence wasn't the same. The Apostles didn't get to look in Jesus' eyes and hear his voice anymore. But it was real. It is real. Jesus continues to be really and truly present in the Church, and it's there, more than any place, that we come to know him. He is there in the proclamation of the Gospel, and he is there in the celebration of the sacraments.

We also come to know Jesus in prayer. When we call on Jesus as our Savior, when we meditate upon his life in the Scriptures or in the Rosary, or when we spend time in silent reflection after receiving his Body and Blood in Communion, we come to know him intimately, not just as our Lord and master and teacher but as a friend:

> You are my friends if you do what I command you. No longer do I call you servants, for the servant does not know what his master is doing; but I have called you friends, for all that I have heard from my Father I have made known to you. (John 15:14–15)

SELECTED READING

Ralph Martin, *The Fulfillment of All Desire*, pp. 122–123

John of the Cross makes the point that sensual attractions are so strong and so rooted in our nature that efforts of renunciation by themselves will not be totally successful. A greater attraction, a greater love has to inflame us in order to enable us to let go of lesser, disordered loves. . . .

One of the main ways we open ourselves for this greater love to possess us is through prayer. We need to remember though that the spiritual life is not primarily about certain practices of piety and techniques of prayer, but about a relationship. It's about responding to the One who has created and redeemed us, and who loves us with a love stronger than death, a love that desires to raise us from the dead. Much that is true of human relationships is also true of our relationship with God. Human relationships of friendship or marriage need time, attention, and care for them to continue and to grow. The same is true of our relationship with God. We have been called to union but we need to respond. As we turn to God in conversion or in a deeper awakening, besides turning away from deliberate sin—which deforms the soul, blocks the relationship and offends the Person who has sacrificed His life for us—we need to positively build the relationship by paying attention to the One who loves us. Prayer is at root simply paying attention to God. All the saints speak of its importance.

Thérèse speaks of the power and simplicity of prayer.

> How great is the power of Prayer! . . . I say very simply to God what I wish to say, without composing beautiful sentences, and He always understands me.

> For me, prayer is an aspiration of the heart, it is a simple glance directed to heaven, it is a cry of gratitude and love in the midst of trial as well as joy; finally, it is something great, supernatural, which expands my soul and unites me to Jesus.

Teresa of Avila tells us that the entrance into the mansions (or stages) of the spiritual journey begins with prayer. Francis de Sales tells us that while the struggle against sin is crucial, even more so is prayer.

> Since prayer places our intellect in the brilliance of God's light and exposes our will to the warmth of his heavenly love, nothing else so effectively purifies our intellect of ignorance and our will of depraved affections. . . . I especially counsel you to practice mental prayer, the prayer of the heart, and particularly that which centers on the life and passion of our Lord. By often turning your eyes on him in meditation, your whole soul will be filled with him. You will learn his ways and form your actions after the pattern of his.

Bernard concurs:

> But I must insist that we can only dare to undertake either of these things [turning from sin, turning to God] by grace, not by nature, nor even by effort. It is wisdom which overcomes malice, not effort or nature. There is no difficulty in finding grounds for hope: the soul must turn to the Word.

QUESTIONS FOR REVIEW

1. What is prayer?
2. How did God publicly speak to humanity?
3. Why are we able to have a personal relationship with God?
4. How can we hear God's voice in prayer?
5. How does prayer put us in relation with all three members of the Trinity?

QUESTIONS FOR DISCUSSION

1. Do you pray regularly? Why or why not?
2. Is it easy or difficult for you to share your feelings with God? Explain.
3. What are some of the things you talk to your family and friends about? Do you talk to God about those things as well? Why or why not?

Chapter 2

Sources, Guides, and Expressions of Prayer

The Centrality of Scripture to Prayer

As we learned above, prayer is a conversation with God that requires that we listen to how he has spoken to us in divine Revelation. The Scriptures are one of our surest guides for prayer—containing examples and teachings that show us how to pray. They also are a source for prayer: they are God's Word, which comes alive for us in prayer.

Models of Prayer in the Old Testament

> **Assigned Reading**
> Genesis 18:20–33
> Psalm 145

The story of God's relationship with Israel in the Old Testament teaches us more than history. It also teaches us about how our relationship with God unfolds in prayer. As he did with the people of Israel, God calls us, tells us to trust him, and asks us to go on a journey.

1. Adam and Eve

Scripture affirms that God initiates contact with humanity over and over again, beginning with the first pages of Genesis. In the Garden of Eden, Adam and Eve enjoyed a perfect communion with God; they spoke with him and knew him. But then, after they ate the fruit from the tree of the knowledge of good and evil, they hid themselves from God. They knew that they had disobeyed God, and they were ashamed. That, however, didn't stop God from reaching out to them. As the Scriptures tell us, God sought them out: "the Lord God called to the man, and said to him, 'Where are you?'" and "What is this that you have done?" (Gen 3:9, 13). God reached out to find Adam and Eve in their shame and disgrace, just as he does with each of us.

2. Abraham

After the Fall, humanity's communion with God was damaged; our access to God was limited. People couldn't see and know God as Adam and Eve had in the Garden of Eden and, just as it happens to so many of us, the less they spoke with him and the less time they spent with him the further away from God they fell.

God, however, didn't give up. He continued to call people to him, and some—such as Abel and Noah—responded to that call. Abraham in particular was able to respond because his heart was open to hearing God's voice and submissive to it (see Part II, Chapter 2). This attitude is essential to prayer; without it, our prayers are just words.

Abraham responded obediently to God's call, and first expressed his prayer in deeds rather than words. He set off on a journey as God commanded, then built altars to God at each stage of his journey (CCC 2570). Later, his prayers became words too. Abraham's first vocal prayer to God was actually a complaint (Gen 15:2). He pointed out that God didn't seem to be fulfilling the promises he had made (Gen 15:2–3). What's important to note here is that Abraham felt free to honestly express his disappointment to God. This testing of our trust in God's faithfulness is something we experience in prayer as well (CCC 2570). Any questions, confusion, or doubts that we may have are not reasons to turn away from God, but can be part of the substance of our prayer life, as they were for Abraham. We can bring all of these things to God.

We see another aspect of prayer when Abraham learns that God plans to destroy Sodom and Gomorrah. Abraham approaches God humbly and respectfully, but also persistently, to save the cities "For the sake of ten" righteous men (Gen 18:32). He negotiates with God, reminding God of his goodness. This type of prayer is intercession, in which the believer prays for the wants and needs of someone else. It is natural in prayer to turn to God not just for our own needs but for the desires and needs of the people around us. Abraham prayed "with bold confidence" because he understood God's compassion for Israel (CCC 2571). We can do the same.

3. Moses

The most striking example of intercessory prayer in the Old Testament is found in Moses. God, as he did with Abraham, reaches out to Moses, initiating contact with him by calling from the burning bush. God asks Moses to cooperate in his work of saving his people, but Moses hesitates. He is dismayed to be chosen by God and responds saying, "Oh, my Lord, send, I pray, some other person" (Exod 4:13). Moses' objections are instructive for us because they are so utterly human. He is struck dumb with intimidation and feelings of unworthiness, and he doesn't agree to do what God asks without seriously considering and even objecting. But through this dialogue and questioning, Moses truly learns how pray, and God reveals his name to him (Exod 3; CCC 2576).

The Scriptures say that "the Lord used to speak to Moses face to face, as a man speaks to his friend" (Exod 33:11). Throughout Exodus, we see Moses conversing with God. From these times of prayer, he gets the strength and guidance to remain faithful to the mission God had given him to lead and intercede for the people.

Also, like Abraham interceding with God for the inhabitants of Sodom and Gomorrah, Moses prays for the people of Israel to God. When the Israelites turn against God and make a golden calf to worship, Moses boldly asks God not to punish the Israelites (Exod 32:11–14). Like Abraham, Moses argues with God—and God hears his prayer. The boldness of Moses' prayer, based on his confidence in God's love and his righteousness and consistency, inspires the intercessors that followed Moses in Israel and in the Church. Likewise, as the mediator between God and Israel, Moses prefigures Jesus, who is the one mediator between God and men (CCC 2577).

4. David, Solomon, and the Temple

God revealed to Moses the plans for the ark of the covenant and the tabernacle, which would be both God's dwelling place among Israel and the center of their life of prayer and worship. After Israel settled in the Promised Land and the kingdom was established, David, as the king of Israel, prayed on behalf of the people like Moses. Seeing that he lived in a rich palace, while God still dwelled in a tent, David wanted to build a permanent place of worship in Jerusalem, but God wouldn't allow it. This task fell to his son, Solomon.

Once complete, the Temple of Jerusalem replaced the tabernacle as God's dwelling place. The ark of the covenant was located there, and sacrifice and prayer were offered there, led by the priests and kings. The temple was destroyed when Babylon conquered Jerusalem and sent the people into exile, but it was rebuilt after the exile (although the ark of the covenant was lost and never recovered). This second temple was remodeled and expanded greatly by King Herod. This was the temple that stood in the time of Jesus (CCC 2578–2580).

Although all have either disappeared or been destroyed, the ark, the tabernacle, and the temple still remind us that God wants to dwell in our midst. As such, they foreshadowed our churches, where Jesus dwells in the tabernacle and where the sacrifice he offered on Calvary is re-presented every day in the Mass. Just as the temple stood at the heart of Israel's worship of God, the Eucharist offered in our churches stands at the heart of our worship today.

5. The Prophets

Through pilgrimages, feasts, and sacrifices, the people of Israel learned to pray. Sometimes, however, they lost sight of the interior aspect of prayer and worship that needs to accompany ritual. In these times, God sent the prophets to call the people back to faith and repentance (CCC 2581).

Among the prophets, Elijah stands out as a model of prayer. In 1 Kings 18:20–40, he confronts the prophets of Baal and challenges them to a spiritual dual, trusting with utter fidelity that the God of the Israelites was the one true God and would honor his prayers. Like Moses, Elijah and the other prophets remind us to seek God out in solitude and trust that from our encounters with God in prayer we will find the strength we need to carry out his mission for us (CCC 2583–2584).

6. The Psalms

The prayer life of Israel is revealed especially in the Psalms. The Book of Psalms is the Old Testament's "masterwork of prayer" (CCC 2585). It is a treasury of 150 hymns that were used by Israel in their synagogues and at the celebration of the great feasts in Jerusalem. The Psalms contain a wide variety of prayers, both individual and communal, expressing every emotion and spiritual state: despair and confidence in God, sorrow for sin, and rejoicing in triumph. They also contain Israel's reflection on and thanksgiving for God's work in their history, and they look forward to the coming of the Messiah and the ushering in of God's kingdom. Consequently, the Psalms continue to teach us how to pray and are central to the worship of the Church.

Jesus Shows Us How to Pray

> **Assigned Reading**
> Psalm 22

The examples of prayer found in the Old Testament are illuminated by the example of Jesus in the New Testament. He is the ultimate model of prayer, prefigured by the priests, prophets, and kings of the Old Testament.

"He Withdrew to a Deserted Place"

Jesus often made the effort to go to a quiet, private place to pray (Matt 14:13; Mark 1:35; Luke 4:42; 5:16), and he responds negatively toward those who pray "at the street corners," extolling us to pray in private (Matt 6:5–6). Jesus is certainly not against public prayer—he is often found at public worship in the synagogues and the temple (Luke 4:16; John 6:59; Mark 12:35)—but, like the prophets, he reminds us that our public acts of prayer and worship need to be an authentic representation of our inner life of prayer. Jesus wouldn't stand for the hypocrisy of prayer offered for the sake of show or for saving one's reputation, and he shows by example the need to take time to develop our relationship with God alone.

Effective Simplicity

Jesus also stressed the importance of simple, trusting prayer, reminding us that "your Father knows what you need before you ask him" (Matt 6:8). Often we approach God with the idea that we need to convince him to give us what we think we need. In the Our Father (Matt 6:9–13), however, Jesus teaches us to pray the simple words "give us this day our daily bread," that is, give us what we truly *need* each day, which is not necessarily the same as what we *want* or think we need.

Jesus likewise reminds us, "do not be anxious about your life, what you shall eat, nor about your body, what you shall put on. For life is more than food, and the body more than clothing.... Instead, seek his kingdom, and these things shall be yours as well" (Luke 12:22–23, 31). With these words, Jesus reveals a God who is intensely concerned with providing for his children. This reminds us that we shouldn't address God as if he were distant and uncaring, but rather as our Father, who looks after what we truly need.

Intense Abandonment

Even with all the helps we have at our disposal, a relationship with God isn't always easy. He rarely explains the struggles and sorrows of our life to us, so we have to work on accepting difficult circumstances with faith. No one knew this better than Jesus. His prayer in the Garden of Gethsemane was intensely passionate and personal. Humanly speaking, he didn't want to suffer any more than we do, so accepting his coming

Passion required him to submit his own will entirely to the Father's will; he prayed, "My Father, if it be possible, let this chalice pass from me; nevertheless, not as I will, but as you will" (Matt 26:39). Faced with the suffering of the Cross, Jesus revealed his human fear. He has a human will like ours, and he experienced the human emotions we experience. What made the difference for him is that his human will was perfectly united with his divine will. His humble trust and union of will with the Father allowed him to pray that the Father's will be done first.

This union of Jesus' divine will and human will is a great mystery. It is also a lesson for us that is further deepened by his prayer from the Cross, "My God, my God, why have you forsaken me?" (Matt 27:46). Even in his intense agony, Jesus quotes the Scripture. From the Cross he prays Psalm 22, a psalm of an innocent man whose forsakenness is turned into a victory by God. In his union with the Father and trust in him, he faces the suffering of the Cross knowing that that Father will vindicate him and he will triumph even over death.

All Our Life Can Be Lived as a Prayer

By looking at Jesus' life, we see that prayer is not an isolated and private event. Like Moses and Elijah, Jesus' private prayer fueled his public prayer and active ministry. In fact, because he lived every moment of his life in perfect communion with the Father, glorifying him with everything he did, every word, action, miracle, and teaching of Jesus' can be considered a prayer. In this way, prayer can be thought of as a unifying point for all of life, bringing all our actions together and directing them toward God's glory. When it comes to prayer and the rest of our life, there should be no compartmentalization. Our lives should be permeated by prayer, so that our prayer is not just expressed in spoken or thought words to God, but in our entire attitude of life. A life lived in, with, and for God becomes itself a form of prayer—a raising of our minds and hearts to God.

Prayer, Teaching, and Sacraments in the Church

The Apostles and the early Church understood the importance of prayer to true discipleship. The Acts of the Apostles summarizes the life of the first Christians: "they held steadfastly to the apostles' teaching and fellowship, to the breaking of the bread and to the prayers" (Acts 2:42).

Learning, prayer, and the Eucharist were inseparable activities in the life of the early Church. This shows the intimate connection between theology, prayer, and the Eucharist. We simply can't understand the truths of the faith (theology) apart from a life of prayer and sacramental participation. Theology isn't just an academic exercise to "figure out" God, like an equation in mathematics or science. It's a vital part of coming to know God, and it flows out of a living relationship with God.

As we learned in Part III, such a relationship is centered on prayer and the celebration of the sacraments, especially the Eucharist. Our prayer life and our sacramental life mutually reinforce one another. A rich prayer life needs to be nourished by faithful Sunday Mass attendance and worthy reception of Holy Communion. Likewise, the Eucharist and other sacraments will benefit us most if we have a habit of daily prayer and if we approach them in prayer. We do this by preparing ourselves in prayer before receiving Communion or any other sacrament, asking God to bless us through the sacrament and make it bear fruit in our lives. We also do it by reflecting prayerfully after receiving the sacrament, giving thanks to God for what we've just been given. Finally, we do it by participating attentively in the liturgy, offering our hearts and minds to God by joining them with the prayer of the whole Church.

Praying the Scriptures

The Scriptures, however, are not just a guide that teaches us how to pray. They also are a source of prayer; they give us words meant to be prayed.

Praying the Scriptures with the Church

We see this in many forms of prayer in the Church. The Scriptures are used extensively in the liturgy, which is the public prayer of the Church. In the Liturgy of the Hours, which is prayed daily by priests, deacons, religious brothers and sisters, and many laypeople, the Church prays the Psalms and canticles of Scripture, making these prayers and hymns of ancient Israel and the early Church her own today.

Likewise, the Scriptures are read in the Liturgy of the Word at Mass and prayed throughout its entirety, woven into all the various prayers that make up the Mass. From "Glory to God in the highest," which repeats the hymn of the angels proclaiming the birth of Jesus,[1] to "Behold, the Lamb of God" and "Lord, I am not worthy to have you come under my roof," which echo the words of John the Baptist and the centurion,[2] and much more, the whole of the Mass is soaked with Scripture.

Praying the Scriptures on Our Own

One of the prayers in the liturgy that comes directly from Scripture is the Lord's Prayer or "Our Father," which Jesus gave to his disciples when they asked him how to pray (Matt 6:9–13). We pray this prayer outside the liturgy as well, especially when we pray the Rosary. Like the Mass, the Rosary is a prayer that incorporates the words of Scripture. In addition to the Our Father, the other major prayer of the Rosary, the Hail Mary, has us greet and praise the Blessed Mother using the words of the Archangel Gabriel and Elizabeth from Luke 1:28 and Luke 1:42. Also, like the Mass, the Rosary is a way of praying the Scriptures, because in it we meditate on the central events of the Bible: the mysteries of the life of Jesus.

Another traditional prayer that has its roots in Scripture is the Angelus:

---

1 Order of Mass, 8; Luke 2:14.

2 Order of Mass, 132; John 1:29; Matt 8:8.

The Angelus

V. The Angel of the Lord declared unto Mary:
R. And she conceived of the Holy Spirit.
Hail Mary . . .
V. Behold the handmaid of the Lord,
R. Be it done unto me according to your Word.
Hail Mary . . .
V. And the Word was made flesh,
R. And dwelt among us.
Hail Mary . . .
V. Pray for us, O holy Mother of God,
R. That we may be made worthy of the promises of Christ.
Let us pray:
Pour forth, we beseech you, O Lord, your grace into our hearts: that we, to whom the Incarnation of Christ your Son was made known by the message of an Angel, may by his Passion and Cross be brought to the glory of his Resurrection. Through the same Christ Our Lord.
Amen.[3]

Similar to the Rosary, the Angelus is a prayer to Mary that draws from Scripture for its words, and it calls us to meditate on a series of events in the lives of Jesus and Mary: the Annunciation of the Archangel Gabriel to Mary, Mary's yes to God's will, and the Incarnation of the Son of God in her womb. In addition to the quotes from Luke 1:28 and Luke 1:42 in the Hail Mary, it depicts the rest of the scene of the Annunciation from Luke 1:26–38, quoting Mary's response in Luke 1:38, and proclaiming the mystery of the Incarnation that occurred with the words of John 1:14, "And the Word became flesh and dwelt among us."

---

[3] United States Conference of Catholic Bishops, "Angelus," http://www.usccb.org/prayer-and-worship/prayers-and-devotions/prayers/angelus.cfm.

Lectio Divina

The Scriptures are the Word of God. They inspire our prayers in the liturgy and devotions like the Rosary, but we should also approach them prayerfully when we read them on our own, ready to hear God's voice:

> Prayer should accompany the reading of Sacred Scripture, so that God and man may talk together; for "we speak to Him when we pray; we hear Him when we read the divine saying."[4]

Reading through the Scriptures or other spiritual writings prayerfully is a great way to engage in prayer. This kind of meditative reading is called *lectio divina*, or "divine reading." Peter Kreeft states:

> *Lectio divina*, "divine reading," is a method of private prayer used and recommended by the Church since ancient times. It is simply reading Scripture as prayer, reading Scripture in God's presence, praying verse by verse, sentence by sentence, or word by word, slowly and thoughtfully, letting the words of Scripture suggest themes of prayer. This is both one of the best ways of praying and one of the best ways of reading Scripture, especially the Psalms and the Gospels. "The Church 'forcefully and specially exhorts all the Christian faithful . . . to learn "the surpassing knowledge of Jesus Christ" (Phil 3:8) by frequent reading of the divine Scriptures. . . . Let them remember, however, that prayer should accompany the reading of Sacred Scripture, so that a dialogue takes place between God and man'" (CCC 2653).[5]

Lectio divina is the internalizing of the "God-breathed" words of Scripture so that they become a prayer. It developed out of the practice of daily spiritual reading practiced by monks and nuns since the early

---

[4] *Dei Verbum*, §25.

[5] Peter Kreeft, *Catholic Christianity: A Complete Catechism of Catholic Beliefs Based on the Catechism of the Catholic Church* (San Francisco: Ignatius Press, 2001), 385.

centuries of the Church,[6] but many lay people practice it as well. Sometimes it is broken down into a four-part method consisting of reading (*lectio*), meditation (*meditatio*), prayer (*oratio*), and contemplation (*contemplatio*). However, it is not necessary to follow a strict method. You can pray the Scriptures just by reading them prayerfully and with care, placing yourself in the scene or reflecting on how the words apply to your life, and letting these thoughts move you to pray to God and give him thanks.

Expressions of Prayer

All prayer is a raising of the heart to God, but every believer responds to God's invitation differently, so this raising of the heart can be expressed in many ways. Christian Tradition has particularly recognized three primary expressions of prayer: vocal prayer, meditation, and contemplation (CCC 2699).

Vocal Prayer

It can go without saying that prayer can be vocal. We know from our experience in and out of church that we pray out loud. But what does it mean to pray with our voices? From infancy we make noise with our vocal cords to communicate. We learn to speak in words and phrases to communicate our ever deeper and more complex needs, from hunger and tiredness to fear, anxiety, and love. We spend our lives engaged in conversation with others, and it's so natural and authentically human to speak aloud. Consider this in the light of the prologue of the Gospel of John:

> In the beginning was the Word, and the Word was with God, and the Word was God. He was in the beginning with God; all

[6] Saint Benedict, Abbot of Monte Cassino, *The Holy Rule of Saint Benedict* (London: Thomas Richardson and Son, 1865), chap. 48.

> things were made through him, and without him was not anything made that was made. In him was life, and the life was the light of men. The light shines in the darkness, and the darkness has not overcome it. (John 1:1–5)

John calls Jesus "the Word" (in Greek, *Logos*). According to John, God speaks his Word, and through the Word, creation comes into being. That creation unfolds and brings the light of God into the world. This gets at a key element of speech communication: speech removes doubt and darkness. We speak in order to clarify the truth, and we speak to make ourselves known clearly.

Just as speech is necessary to human survival and thriving, vocal prayer is necessary to spiritual growth and holiness. While prayer is defined by the inner movement of the heart toward God, as bodily beings, with voices and ears, it's fitting that the content of our hearts should be expressed outwardly in words. In this way, we pray with our whole being—body and spirit—and we also are able to pray with others. In doing so, we follow the example of Jesus, who prayed vocally in the synagogue with friends, family, and strangers, and in private by himself (CCC 2700–2704).

Mental Prayer

As vocal prayer is natural to humanity, so too is the natural progression to non-verbal means of communication. Have you had the experience of being with a close family member or friend and being able to communicate with him or her with a look or body language, or even knowing what he or she was going to say intuitively? We can and often do communicate silently because of our deep knowledge of those close to us. This gives us a glimpse into internal or mental prayer: meditation and contemplation.

Meditation

Meditation, properly speaking, is active mental prayer:

> Meditation engages thought, imagination, emotion, and desire. This mobilization of faculties is necessary in order to deepen our convictions of faith, prompt the conversion of our heart, and strengthen our will to follow Christ. (CCC 2708)

Meditation requires concentration and commitment that can be difficult to sustain, but there are many things that can help us. First among these are the Scriptures and other spiritual books. As previously mentioned, meditation is a central part of *lectio divina*. Engaging the drama of Scripture or a spiritual work with our minds, imagination, and emotions allows us to enter into the scene as a character. We get a chance to react to the situations and engage the other characters. In this way we get to learn about ourselves in evaluating our reactions, and we open ourselves up to God's presence in his Word (CCC 2705).

In addition to the Scriptures and writings of spiritual authors, we can find inspiration for meditation in the actions and words of the liturgy, in icons and other sacred art, or in God's work in creation, history, and our own lives. If we are humble and faithful, all these things can move our hearts to thoughtful reflection so that we can discover how God might be speaking to us through them and what he wants us to do in response (CCC 2706).

Contemplation

Meditation is of great value in actively engaging our thought, imagination, emotion, and desire, but our prayer can go further—from meditation on the mysteries of Christ to union with Christ himself and the experience of his love in contemplation.

St. Teresa of Ávila (1515–1582), a master of the life of prayer and a doctor of the Church, describes contemplative prayer as "a close sharing between friends; it means taking time frequently to be alone with him who we know loves us."[7] This prayer goes beyond words to let us simply be in God's presence for a time. That's it: contemplation is to make ourselves quiet, "gather up" our hearts, and sit in silence and spend time with God. It's like when a married couple just sits together, holding hands, or when a baby rests silently in her mother's arms. It's a time of profound communion and rest.

This sounds simple, but it's not always so easy. It requires making time for the Lord and a firm determination not to give up in seeking to know him. When thoughts, boredom, distractions, or emotions pull our mind in many directions, we need to allow God to pull our will back to silence and recollection. Then the Holy Spirit can continue pouring his love into our hearts.

Just like a human relationship where we only grow through the process of building trust and openness, contemplative prayer is only possible if we make ourselves vulnerable to God. In doing so, we allow God into our souls in a deeper, more profound way. This involves effort on our part, but ultimately, contemplation is a grace that God gives. This is an important point: all prayer involves both our own effort and God's grace. We cooperate with God's grace in willing acceptance of his invitation to spiritual growth, and this cooperation makes the experience of God's love in contemplative prayer an attainable goal (CCC 2713).

SELECTED READING

Pope Benedict XVI, Encyclical Letter on the Life and Mission of the Church *Verbum Domini* (September 30, 2010), nos. 86–87

The Synod frequently insisted on the need for a prayerful approach to the sacred text as a fundamental element in the spiritual life of every believer, in the various ministries and states in life, with par-

[7] St. Teresa of Jesus, *The Book of Her Life*, 8.5, in *The Collected Works of St. Teresa of Avila*, trans. K. Kavanaugh, OCD, and O. Rodriguez, OCD (Washington DC: Institute of Carmelite Studies, 1976), I, 67, quoted in CCC 2709.

ticular reference to *lectio divina*. The word of God is at the basis of all authentic Christian spirituality. The Synod Fathers thus took up the words of the Dogmatic Constitution *Dei Verbum*: "Let the faithful go gladly to the sacred text itself, whether in the sacred liturgy, which is full of the divine words, or in devout reading, or in such suitable exercises and various other helps which, with the approval and guidance of the pastors of the Church, are happily spreading everywhere in our day. Let them remember, however, that prayer should accompany the reading of sacred Scripture." The Council thus sought to reappropriate the great patristic tradition, which had always recommended approaching the Scripture in dialogue with God. As Saint Augustine puts it: "Your prayer is the word you speak to God. When you read the Bible, God speaks to you; when you pray, you speak to God."

Origen, one of the great masters of this way of reading the Bible, maintains that understanding Scripture demands, even more than study, closeness to Christ and prayer. Origen was convinced, in fact, that the best way to know God is through love, and that there can be no authentic *scientia Christi* apart from growth in his love. In his *Letter to Gregory*, the great Alexandrian theologian gave this advice: "Devote yourself to the *lectio* of the divine Scriptures; apply yourself to this with perseverance. Do your reading with the intent of believing in and pleasing God. If during the *lectio* you encounter a closed door, knock and it will be opened to you by that guardian of whom Jesus said, 'The gatekeeper will open it for him.' By applying yourself in this way to *lectio divina*, search diligently and with unshakable trust in God for the meaning of the divine Scriptures, which is hidden in great fullness within. You ought not, however, to be satisfied merely with knocking and seeking: to understand the things of God, what is absolutely necessary is *oratio*. For this reason, the Saviour told us not only: 'Seek and you will find,' and 'Knock and it shall be opened to you,' but also added, 'Ask and you shall receive.'"

In this regard, however, one must avoid the risk of an individualistic approach, and remember that God's word is given to us precisely to build communion, to unite us in the Truth along our path to God. While it is a word addressed to each of us personally, it is also a word which builds community, which builds the Church. Consequently, the sacred text must always be approached in the communion of the Church. In effect, "a communal reading of Scripture is extremely important, because the living subject in the sacred Scriptures is the People of God, it is the Church. . . . Scripture does not belong to the past, because its subject, the People of God inspired by God himself, is always the same, and therefore the word is always alive in the living subject. As such, it is important to read and experience sacred Scripture in communion with the Church, that is, with all the great witnesses to this word, beginning with the earliest Fathers up to the saints of our own day, up to the present-day magisterium." . . .

The documents produced before and during the Synod mentioned a number of methods for a faith-filled and fruitful approach to sacred Scripture. Yet the greatest attention was paid to *lectio divina*, which is truly "capable of opening up to the faithful the treasures of God's word, but also of bringing about an encounter with Christ, the living word of God." I would like here to review the basic steps of this procedure.

It opens with the reading (*lectio*) of a text, which leads to a desire to understand its true content: *what does the biblical text say in itself?* Without this, there is always a risk that the text will become a pretext for never moving beyond our own ideas. Next comes meditation (*meditatio*), which asks: *what does the biblical text say to us?* Here, each person, individually but also as a member of the community, must let himself or herself be moved and challenged. Following this comes prayer (*oratio*), which asks the question: *what do we say to the Lord in response to his word?* Prayer, as petition, intercession, thanksgiving and praise, is the primary way by which the word transforms us. Finally, *lectio divina* concludes with contemplation (*contemplatio*), during which we take up, as a gift from God, his own way of seeing and judging reality, and ask ourselves *what conversion of mind, heart and life is the Lord asking of us?* In the Letter to the Romans, Saint Paul tells us: "Do not be conformed to this world, but be transformed by the renewal of your mind, that you may prove what is the will of God, what is good and acceptable and perfect" (12:2). . . .

> Contemplation aims at creating within us a truly wise and discerning vision of reality, as God sees it, and at forming within us "the mind of Christ" (1 *Cor* 2:16). The word of God appears here as a criterion for discernment: it is "living and active, sharper than any two-edged sword, piercing to the division of soul and spirit, of joints and marrow, and discerning the thoughts and intentions of the heart" (*Heb* 4:12). We do well also to remember that the process of *lectio divina* is not concluded until it arrives at action (*actio*), which moves the believer to make his or her life a gift for others in charity.

QUESTIONS FOR REVIEW

1. Who are two exemplary models of prayer in the Old Testament? What is one lesson we can learn from each?
2. What book of the Bible is filled with prayerful songs that we should continue to pray today?
3. Name two important lessons Jesus taught us about prayer.
4. What is an ancient method of praying using Scripture? Describe it.
5. What are the four different expressions of prayer?

QUESTIONS FOR DISCUSSION

1. Of all the Old Testament figures named here, which one teaches you a lesson about prayer that you think you need right now? Explain.
2. How could you carve out more time in your day to be alone with God? Is there a particular place you like to pray or would like to go to pray?
3. Do you have a favorite prayer? If so, what is it and what about it do you like?

Chapter 3

Forms and Habits of Prayer

Vocal prayer, meditation, and contemplation are different ways that prayer can be expressed, but we also can examine prayer in terms of its purpose or form. The Catechism defines six different forms of prayer: blessing, adoration, petition, intercession, thanksgiving, and praise.

Forms of Prayer

Blessing

When it comes to prayer, "blessing" has many different meanings. First, we say that *God blesses us* when he favors us and gives us prosperity or particular gifts.

Second, in the language of the Bible, our response to God's blessing is also called blessing. In this sense, we say that *we bless God* in prayer. God is all-powerful and self-sufficient, so he doesn't need "blessings" (i.e., favors and gifts) from us like we need them from him. So, for us to bless God means that we gratefully acknowledge him as the source of blessing, giving him glory, praise, and thanksgiving. This meaning of "bless" is less common in everyday speech, but you hear it in the prayers of the Mass. For example, in the Gloria we sing to God, "we bless you," and at the Offertory, in response to the gifts God has blessed us with, we say, "Blessed be God forever."[1]

Finally, we say that *we bless someone* or *something* when we pray to God to bless a person—giving him the grace and protection and gifts he needs—or a thing—making it holy so that his people may be blessed through it. We also find this kind of blessing in the Mass. At the beginning of the First Eucharistic Prayer, the priest blesses the bread and wine, which will become the Body and Blood of Christ, praying, "accept and bless these gifts," and making the Sign of the Cross over them. Likewise, at the end of Mass, he blesses the people, making the Sign of the Cross and praying, "May almighty God bless you, the Father, and the Son, and the Holy Spirit."[2]

Adoration

Blessing recognizes God as the source of all gifts; adoration more fundamentally recognizes who God is in relation to who we are. Adoration means recognizing our place in the grand scheme of things and orienting ourselves properly before God. This is why the Catechism calls adoration the "first act of the virtue of religion" (CCC 2096). We adore God because he is our Creator. Only God is self-sufficient, and we depend entirely upon him for our existence and salvation. Only he is all-powerful and can deliver us from evil. Understanding these facts leads us to adore him in prayer. Adoration is a prayer of complete submission to the all-powerful God, who responds to our humility by raising us up to share in his very life (see 2 Pet 1:4). Adoring the God of love in humility, we are filled with confidence that he will hear our prayers (CCC 2628).

Petition

Petition—asking God for things—is probably the most basic and familiar form of prayer. In blessing and adoration, we recognize that we depend

---

1 Order of Mass, 8, 23, 25.

2 Order of Mass, 84, 141.

upon God for everything we have and are. The prayer of petition grows naturally out of this. Knowing that God loves us and that we rely upon him for all we need, we turn to him, trusting that he will take care of those needs.

Recall that Jesus taught us to pray, trusting that "your Father knows what you need before you ask him" (Matt 6:8; see Chapter 3). Of course, this raises the question: if God already knows what we need, why do we have to ask him for it? The answer is that prayers of petition express our relationship with God and our trust in him. When we ask God for things, we acknowledge our neediness and dependence on him and his greatness and concern for us. God wants us to ask him for things so that we can grow in our relationship with him and our trust in him (CCC 2629).

When blessing and adoration move us to prayers of petition, we see that the first thing we need from God is his forgiveness. So, recognizing God's holiness and our sinfulness (and trusting humbly in his mercy), the first thing we ask for in petition is pardon for our sins. This helps our prayer to flow from a humble and clean heart and is why the first prayer of petition at Mass is the Penitential Rite, where we confess our sinfulness and ask God to prepare us to celebrate the sacred mysteries of the Eucharist by having mercy on our sins. We confess that we have sinned and cry out, "Lord, have mercy," "Christ, have mercy."[3]

When we approach God with prayers of petition, it's also important to pray for the spread of the kingdom of God. Thus, in the Our Father we pray, "Thy kingdom come." By praying for the coming of the kingdom and for everything we need to welcome and cooperate with its coming, we collaborate with the whole Church in the mission of Jesus and Holy Spirit (CCC 2632).

At the same time, the fact that our prayers are directed toward this ultimate goal doesn't mean that we should hesitate to ask God for things that seem small or minor:

> When we share in God's saving love, we understand that *every need* can become the object of petition. Christ, who assumed all

---

[3] Order of Mass, 4; CCC 2631.

> things in order to redeem all things, is glorified by what we ask the Father in his name [Cf. *Jn* 14:13]. It is with this confidence that St. James and St. Paul exhort us to pray *at all times* [Cf. *Jas* 1:5–8; *Eph* 5:20; *Phil* 4:6–7; *Col* 3:16–17; *1 Thess* 5:17–18]. (CCC 2633)

Intercession

Intercession is prayer of petition on behalf of others. In Chapter 3 we saw how Abraham and Moses interceded for others in the Old Testament, prefiguring Jesus, who is the one mediator between God and men, "the one intercessor with the Father on behalf of all men, especially sinners" (CCC 2634). If our hearts are attentive to God's mercy, we will be moved to intercede for others, just like Abraham and Moses, and in doing so, we participate in the intercession of Christ.

Intercessory prayer is an important expression of the communion of saints, the sharing of spiritual goods that exists between all members of the Church—on earth, in purgatory, and in heaven. We intercede for our brothers and sisters in Christ on earth and awaiting heaven in purgatory, and the saints in heaven intercede for us (CCC 2635). In this way we practice our love for one another. Recall Jesus' words, "By this all men will know that you are my disciples, if you have love for one another" (John 13:35).

Our prayer of intercession, however, isn't limited just to those who are close to us or to our fellow Christians. The Church prays for nations, for rulers, and for all peoples (especially in the Prayers of the Faithful at Mass), and Jesus commands us to even pray for those who hate and persecute us.[4]

---

[4] Matt 5:44; *General Instruction of the Roman Missal,* (Washington, D.C: United States Conference of Catholic Bishops, 2003), 69–71; CCC 2636.

Thanksgiving

Acknowledging our dependence on God for our needs in petition and intercession leads us to give him thanks for everything he has given us. "As in the prayer of petition, every event and need can become an offering of thanksgiving" (CCC 2638).

Thanksgiving is an essential part of a relationship with God in prayer, and it's central to the life of the Church. The thanksgiving of the Church is expressed above all in the Eucharist. In fact, the word "Eucharist" comes from the Greek word *eucharisteō*, which means "give thanks." In the Mass, we give thanks to God for all his blessings, symbolized by the bread and wine we offer. Our humble offerings of thanksgiving are then taken up by Jesus, who turns them into his Body and Blood. In this way, we participate in his great offering of thanksgiving—the work of salvation, in which he "sets creation free from sin and death to consecrate it anew and make it return to the Father, for his glory" (CCC 2637).

Praise

Giving thanks to God leads us naturally to praise him and give him glory, not just for what he does for us, but above all simply because he is God. Praise is closely connected to blessing and adoration, so in a way, the forms of prayer begin and end with God. God blesses us, and we bless him and others in turn; we adore him because we are his creatures, and because we depend on him, we petition him for our needs and we intercede for others; then we give him thanks for creating us and caring for us; and finally we are moved to praise him for his great glory. Thus, the Catechism says, "Praise embraces the other forms of prayer and carries them toward him who is its source and goal: the 'one God, the Father, from whom are all things and for whom we exist' [*1 Cor* 8:6]" (CCC 2639).

We need to use all these forms of prayer. While we might sometimes use just one form on its own—for example, a short prayer of petition when a need confronts us or a short prayer of thanksgiving when something good happens—they are most often combined, and we naturally find ourselves moving between them. As we've seen, all of these forms of prayer can be found in the liturgy:

> The Eucharist contains and expresses all forms of prayer: it is "the pure offering" of the whole Body of Christ to the glory of God's name [Cf. *Mal* 1:11] and, according to the traditions of East and West, it is *the* "sacrifice of praise." (CCC 2643)

Challenges to Prayer

Prayer is not always easy. Difficulties inevitably arise whenever we try to deepen our relationship with God in prayer. For this reason, prayer is a "spiritual battle" that requires effort and commitment (CCC 2725).

Distraction

The first difficulty we face in prayer is distraction. We want to pray, but thoughts and cares come into our mind, and soon we find ourselves thinking about something completely different. It's natural for the mind to swarm with trivial concerns, thoughts, and items from our "to do" list as soon as we try to settle down to pray, even for a few minutes. The solution to distraction in prayer is simply to turn back our heart to the Lord. In other words, when we catch our mind wandering, rather than getting frustrated or giving up, we just need to patiently turn our attention back to our prayer (CCC 2729).

Depending on our state of mind, it may be necessary to do this over and over again, but if we persevere, this exercise can be valuable. As the Catechism points out, "a distraction reveals to us what we are attached to, and this humble awareness before the Lord should awaken our preferential love for him and lead us resolutely to offer him our heart to be purified" (CCC 2729).

In other words, our distractions show us what things we are putting before God—the things of the world that preoccupy us, some of which are legitimate responsibilities and others of which are selfish or trivial concerns. When we choose to turn our mind back to God in prayer, we stir up our love that we might love him with our whole heart, our whole soul, and our whole mind (Matt 22:37), and we offer him our heart so that he can purify it of anything in it that is selfish or sinful.

This battle in prayer against occupation with ourselves requires vigilance or watchfulness. Jesus tells us that we must be alert, keeping watch in prayer for his coming. This means we look forward to the day when Jesus will come again in glory, but it also means that we look for the ways in which Jesus comes to meet us today—in prayer, in the Scriptures, in the Church and the sacraments, and in our neighbor who is in need. To see this, we must be attentive in prayer (CCC 2730).

Spiritual Dryness

If we persevere through distraction and grow in our relationship with God through prayer, we can often find great consolation in it—feelings of peace, contentment, or joy. These feelings can help us through difficult times and encourage us to keep seeking God in prayer. But, even if we are making progress spiritually, these feelings don't always come. We may have times of spiritual dryness when "the heart is separated from God, with no taste for thoughts, memories, and feelings, even spiritual ones" (CCC 2731). We may not understand the reasons why these feelings come and go, but God can bring us through them. In fact, we need to persevere especially in these times when prayer is not enjoyable and comforting. We might feel that there is no one listening when we pray and that prayer is a waste of time. In those moments, though, we need to cling to our prayer, remembering how the suffering of Good Friday and the emptiness of Holy Saturday were followed by the joy of Easter Sunday.

Many saints have experienced this dryness in prayer and have written extensively about the need to keep going to receive deeper intimacy with God. Indeed, St. Teresa of Ávila and St. John of the Cross both discuss dryness as a necessary part of the life of prayer. During these dry times, God is making us ready to receive better gifts. Part of what happens in prayer is that God helps us die to ourselves so that he can unite himself more fully to us: "unless a grain of wheat falls into the earth and dies, it remains alone; but if it dies, it bears much fruit" (John 12:24; see Luke 8:6, 13). Spiritual dryness is meant to lead us to examine ourselves, deepen our conversion, and free us from attachment to fleeting emotions.

Temptations

Several temptations are likely to arise when we try to pray. The most common is simply lack of faith. Because our faith is weak, we have a hard time believing prayer is worthwhile or that God will hear us. Some of us may only turn to God in an emergency or as a last resort. Because of that, we don't really have the peace that comes from a true relationship with God. Even if our prayer is answered, we just go back to our habitual way of acting that caused the problem in the first place. We fail to recognize that we are dependent on God for everything and lack the humility necessary for fruitful prayer (CCC 2732).

This attitude of presumption may lead to another temptation: acedia (sometimes called "sloth"). Acedia is a term the Church Fathers used to describe a kind of spiritual depression that comes from being lax in prayer and careless in our hearts. It can afflict someone who thinks he has reached great spiritual heights, but lacks humility. When discouragement comes, he may find himself falling very hard. Times of discouragement in prayer are meant to remind us of our dependency on God. If we are humble, we will not be surprised by them. They will lead us to deepen our trust in God (CCC 2733).

Trust in Prayer

> **Assigned Reading**
> James 4:1–8

To overcome these difficulties in prayer, we need to trust God, just like Jesus trusted his Father. This trust is tested in these difficulties and temptations—especially in times that we think that God is not hearing our prayers of petition. Why does it sometimes seem like God doesn't hear our prayers? Why is this so difficult for us? The Letter of St. James helps explain this, noting, "You ask and do not receive, because you ask wrongly, to spend it on your passions" (Jas 4:3).

How do we ask wrongly, though? First, it may be that our prayer doesn't seem to be heard because we may not be asking for something that would further God's kingdom or even be good for us. It might be that what we're asking for would actually harm us or that God has something better in mind for us. This means that sometimes God's answer to our prayer may be no.

Second, we may be asking wrongly by praying with the wrong attitude. We ask wrongly if we approach God as if he were a tool for getting what we want rather than our loving Father and Creator, who deserves our thanks, praise, and adoration. When our focus is primarily on the gifts rather than the Giver, we pray with a divided heart—our heart is set more on the things we want rather than on God himself (CCC 2735, 2740).

Effective prayer requires the humility to recognize that when we come before God "we do not know how to pray as we ought" (Rom 8:26). It also requires the trust to recognize that he will answer our prayer in the way that is best for us, even if we cannot see how. The purpose of prayer isn't just to get everything we want but to transform our hearts—to develop our trust in God and bring our will in conformity with his (CCC 2739).

Even if God does not grant the thing we ask for in prayer, when we ask with the right attitude, he responds by transforming our hearts in this way. Our prayer is united with the prayer of Jesus, who always seeks what pleases the Father. Trusting in God, who showed his love for us by saving us through the Passion and Resurrection of his Son, we know that the prayer of Jesus will be heard. God will give us the gifts we need, and above all, he will give us the gift of his Holy Spirit (CCC 2741).

St. Paul exhorts us to pray without ceasing (1 Thess 5:17). With the difficulties and temptations we face, constant prayer like this is only possible if our prayer comes from love. Love opens our hearts to see certain important facts about prayer. These facts include:

- *It is always possible to pray* because our time belongs to God and Christ is with us always.
- *Prayer is necessary for us to survive as disciples* because prayer keeps our hearts close to the Holy Spirit, who leads us and preserves us from falling back into slavery to sin.
- *Prayer is inseparable from Christian life* because prayer comes from and expresses the same love of God and neighbor, which is the basis of our life in Christ (CCC 2742–2745).

The Lord's Prayer

To conclude and summarize our understanding of prayer, let's turn to Jesus' most famous teaching on prayer, the "Our Father" (Matt 6:9–13):

> Our Father who art in heaven,
> Hallowed be thy name.
> Thy kingdom come.
> Thy will be done
>   On earth as it is in heaven.
> Give us this day our daily bread;
> And forgive us our trespasses
>   As we forgive those who trespass against us;
> And lead us not into temptation,
> But deliver us from evil.

The "Lord's Prayer," or the "Our Father," reflects Jesus' teaching on prayer. It's so short and simple that even little children can easily learn it. Like most short, simple payers, it's meant to be repeated. But, through conscientious repetition and practice at prayer in general, a prayer (like this one) that seems simple can gradually reveal profound spiritual depths and become an important aid in our journey to holiness. This is how the Lord's Prayer can form the basis of the Church's understanding of prayer even though it is so simple. In a wonderful way, it lays out how we should pray and everything we should pray for. We can see this more clearly when we break the prayer down and examine its individual parts.

1. *Our Father, who art in heaven*: Here, Jesus teaches us to call God "Father." This is the basis of our prayer. God wants us to approach him, with the trust of a child, as our loving Father (see CCC 2777–2802).
2. *Hallowed be thy name*: This reminds us prayer should begin by honoring God in blessing and adoration, and praying that all people will bless and adore him with us. This fulfills the "first and greatest commandment" to love God with all our heart, soul, and mind (Matt 22:38; Deut 6:4; see CCC 2807–2815).
3. *Thy kingdom come*: With this phrase, Jesus reminds us that the ultimate thing we should ask for in prayer is for the coming of the final victory of God and the ushering in of the "new heaven and new earth" (Rev 21:1). When we do this, our prayer becomes a cooperation in this victory, which will come definitively at the end of time. It also, however, helps bring about the reign of God right now, both in our world and in our hearts (see CCC 2816–2821).
4. *Thy will be done on earth as it is in heaven*: God reigns when his will is done. So we need to pray for God's will to be done on earth just as it is now done in heaven by the angels and saints who adore and obey him perfectly. In prayer, we must seek God's will for our own lives, and we must seek to bring our will in conformity to his so that we can build up the kingdom in our own way according to our vocation (see CCC 2822–2827).
5. *Give us this day our daily bread*: We depend upon God for the graces we need to accomplish his will, and here Jesus reminds us to ask for those graces. This petition refers to our day-to-day needs, both physical and spiritual, but at a deeper level it points toward the Eucharist, for communion with Jesus provides us with the grace we need to do God's will in building up his kingdom (see CCC 2828–2837).
6. *And forgive us our trespasses as we forgive those who trespass against us*: This passage reminds us that when we come before God in prayer, we must recognize our need for forgiveness. We need to implore the mercy of God, asking for the grace to forgive others and fulfill

Christ's command: "You shall love your neighbor as yourself" (Mark 12:31; see CCC 2838–2845).

7. *And lead us not into temptation*: This petition follows from the last one. It's not meant to imply that God tempts us to sin; God by his nature cannot do so. The translation given in the New Revised Standard Version of the Bible, "And do not bring us to the time of trial," is closer to the original Greek. It is more a plea for the grace of help in trials and the grace of trust in God's providential care over our lives (see CCC 2846–2849).
8. *But deliver us from evil*: This final petition that Jesus calls us to make is a prayer of trust that we will not be taken from God's hands. It refers not just to evil in general, but to Satan, the Evil One. We know that Jesus has won the ultimate victory over Satan, so we pray in trust that God will protect us from Satan's power and all evils (CCC 2850–2854).

Essentially, through these eight petitions, the Lord's Prayer functions as a brief catechism on prayer. It provides us with a roadmap of prayer—a roadmap that includes thanksgiving, praise, and repentance. This is why the Church sees it as the consummate prayer and even "the summary of the whole Gospel."[5]

SELECTED READING
St. Francis de Sales, *Introduction to the Devout Life*, pt. II, chap. 1

Prayer opens the understanding to the brightness of Divine Light, and the will to the warmth of Heavenly Love—nothing can so effectually purify the mind from its many ignorances, or the will from its perverse affections. It is as a healing water which causes the roots of our good desires to send forth fresh shoots, which washes away the soul's imperfections, and allays the thirst of passion.

---

[5] Tertullian, *On Prayer* 1, quoted in CCC 2761.

But especially I commend earnest mental prayer to you, more particularly such as bears upon the Life and Passion of our Lord. If you contemplate Him frequently in meditation, your whole soul will be filled with Him, you will grow in His Likeness, and your actions will be moulded on His. He is the Light of the world; therefore in Him, by Him, and for Him we shall be enlightened and illuminated; He is the Tree of Life, beneath the shadow of which we must find rest;—He is the Living Fountain of Jacob's well, wherein we may wash away every stain. Children learn to speak by hearing their mother talk, and stammering forth their childish sounds in imitation; and so if we cleave to the Savior in meditation, listening to His words, watching His actions and intentions, we shall learn in time, through His Grace, to speak, act and will like Himself. Believe me, my child, there is no way to God save through this door. Just as the glass of a mirror would give no reflection save for the metal behind it, so neither could we here below contemplate the Godhead, were it not united to the Sacred Humanity of our Saviour, Whose Life and Death are the best, sweetest and most profitable subjects that we can possibly select for meditation. It is not without meaning that the Saviour calls Himself the Bread come down from Heaven;—just as we eat bread with all manner of other food, so we need to meditate and feed upon our Dear Lord in every prayer and action. His Life has been meditated and written about by various authors. I should specially commend to you the writings of Saint Bonaventura, Bellintani, Bruno, Capilla, Grenada and Da Ponte.

Give an hour every day to meditation before dinner;—if you can, let it be early in the morning, when your mind will be less cumbered, and fresh after the night's rest. Do not spend more than an hour thus, unless specially advised to do so by your spiritual father.

If you can make your meditation quietly in church, it will be well, and no one, father or mother, husband or wife, can object to an hour spent there, and very probably you could not secure a time so free from interruption at home.

Begin all prayer, whether mental or vocal, by an act of the Presence of God. If you observe this rule strictly, you will soon see how useful it is.

It may help you to say the Creed, Lord's Prayer, etc., in Latin, but you should also study them diligently in your own language, so as thoroughly to gather up the meaning of these holy words, which must be used fixing your thoughts steadily on their purport, not striving to say many words so much as seeking to say a few with your whole heart. One Our Father said devoutly is worth more than many prayers hurried over.

The Rosary is a useful devotion when rightly used, and there are various little books to teach this. It is well, too, to say pious Litanies, and the other vocal prayers appointed for the Hours and found in Manuals of devotion,—but if you have a gift for mental prayer, let that always take the chief place, so that if, having made that, you are hindered by business or any other cause from saying your wonted vocal prayers, do not be disturbed, but rest satisfied with saying the Lord's Prayer, the Angelic Salutation, and the Creed after your meditation.

If, while saying vocal prayers, your heart feels drawn to mental prayer, do not resist it, but calmly let your mind fall into that channel, without troubling because you have not finished your appointed vocal prayers. The mental prayer you have substituted for them is more acceptable to God, and more profitable to your soul. I should make an exception of the Church's Offices, if you are bound to say those by your vocation—in such a case these are your duty.

If it should happen that your morning goes by without the usual meditation, either owing to a pressure of business, or from any other cause, (which interruptions you should try to prevent as far as possible,) try to repair the loss in the afternoon, but not immediately after a meal, or you will perhaps be drowsy, which is bad both for your meditation and your health. But if you are unable all day to make up for the omission, you must remedy it as far as may be by ejaculatory prayer, and by reading some spiritual book, together with an act of penitence for the neglect, together with a steadfast resolution to do better the next day.

QUESTIONS FOR REVIEW

1. What are the six forms of prayer?
2. What is an example of each form of prayer?
3. What difficulties can arise in prayer?
4. How do we overcome these difficulties?
5. What prayer is considered a "catechism" on prayer? Explain.

QUESTIONS FOR DISCUSSION

1. Of the six forms of prayer, which forms do you most commonly use? Which don't you use? How could using more forms of prayer deepen your relationship with God?
2. What are some of your most common distractions in prayer? What does this say about what you are attached to and prioritize in life?
3. Is it difficult for you to trust God and persist in prayer? Why or why not?

Appendix

Challenges

Growth in relationships always requires questions. These questions, especially theological ones, are positive signs of growth. We should never be averse to asking questions, especially about God. As men and women, we are naturally inquisitive. It's in our nature to seek the good. We do this because we want to be happy. Just as we cannot be happy without prayer, we cannot be happy without knowing the truth, and that requires looking for answers.

Our modern culture is too often satisfied with surface level answers, the kind of answers you get from googling a question. But questions, especially religious questions, need to be taken more seriously. In this last section, we will look at some common, yet serious, questions concerning Jesus; his saving Passion, death, and Resurrection; and how we apply the grace that comes from that mystery to our lives of faith.

Why Would God the Father Allow His Son to Suffer?

Suffering is something that we as human beings find intolerable, especially when it's suffering inflicted by a fellow human being. When we look at the suffering of Jesus at a surface level, it's easy to feel angry with the Romans who crucified him, the Apostles who abandoned him, and the Jewish leaders who turned him over to be judged. It's also possible to be confused, even scandalized, by God the Father, who allowed the death of his only Son. How could a kind, loving God permit such a thing? This question is often raised as an argument against Christianity, and it is a serious question, which demands a serious response.

In a sense, this question is at the heart of the subject of this entire course—the Paschal Mystery. As we learned in Part I, God created human beings to be holy and enjoy friendship with him, but when our first parents sinned, we lost this original holiness and justice. Because of this original sin, all human beings are born with a wounded nature—we lack the life of grace and are alienated from God.

God, however, didn't leave us in this state of sin and separation from him. In Part II we learned how God, in his love for us, promised us a redeemer and prepared the way for him by gathering a nation, Israel, to himself. Jesus is the fulfillment of his promise. He is the Messiah. He is the Son of God, the Second Person of the Trinity, who became a man to reconcile us to God and destroy the power of sin and death. Jesus' entire life is a mystery of redemption, and every aspect and act of his life was part of his mission to redeem us. In Part III we learned how this mission unfolded in his public ministry, and in Part IV we learned how it culminated in the Paschal Mystery of his death and Resurrection.

How is it possible, though, that our salvation comes from something as terrible as the suffering and death of Jesus? While our redemption through the Cross is a mystery of faith that we can never fully comprehend, in Part IV, Chapter 1, we discussed some of the ways Scripture helps us understand this. Jesus is the Suffering Servant foretold by Isaiah, who offers his life in perfect obedience to God even to the point of suffering death. He *ransoms* us, suffering the consequences of our sin to deliver us from slavery to sin and death. His total offering of himself in obedience is a perfect *sacrifice,* which makes up for the guilt of our sin and disobedience. He is the *Paschal Sacrifice,* the Lamb of God, who takes away the sin of the world, fulfilling all the sacrifices of the Old Testament. Because he is fully God, his offering of himself has the power to overcome our guilt and sin in a way no sacrifice we might offer on our own ever could. Because he is fully human, united to us in our human nature, he can make this offering on our behalf.

Thus, God the Father allowed Jesus to suffer and die because of his great love for us. He did not want us to remain separated from him in sin and death, so he sent Jesus to overcome the power that sin and death have over us, restore us to friendship with him, and give us a share in his divine life so that we can live eternally with him in heaven.

It's important to note, however, that while God the Father *foresaw* Christ's death on the Cross and *allowed* it, he did not *cause* it himself. All the human beings involved immediately in Jesus' death—from Pilate to the chief priests to Judas to the Apostles who abandoned him—acted freely. Jesus' death resulted from their specific sinful choices—though, as Jesus himself said, they did not fully understand what they were doing. Broadly speaking though, the cause of Jesus' death was not just the sinful choices of those immediately involved, but the sins of all humanity—from the sin of our first parents to our own sins.

Thus, it was not God the Father who killed Jesus, but human sin. God the Father allowed it—and Jesus himself accepted it—knowing that he could bring our salvation out of it. Thus, through the Cross, God showed us how serious our sin was—it had so distorted our human nature that we simply could not stand a man without sin. But more importantly, through the Cross, God showed us how great his power and his love are. His love for us is so great that he himself willingly suffered the worst consequences of our sin, and his power is so great that, out of this terrible reality, he brought about our salvation.

Why Are Followers of Jesus Willing to Make Sacrifices and Accept Suffering?

Everyone faces suffering in some form or another, but being a follower of Jesus changes how we understand and deal with suffering. First, as Christians, we understand that this suffering results from living in a fallen world. Because of original sin, suffering is an unavoidable part of the human experience. We can do things to avoid, remove, or relieve some of the suffering in the world, but suffering will always be with us in some form or another.

Second, we respond to suffering by following the example of Jesus. Like Jesus the Good Samaritan, we must reach out in compassion and mercy to alleviate the sufferings of others. This is one way we fulfill our duty to love our neighbors (see Luke 10:29–37). Also, like Jesus the Suffering Servant, we must learn to accept suffering in our own lives with patience and trust in God (see Isa 52:13–53:12).

Jesus tells us that suffering and sacrifice are a necessary part of following him: "If any man would come after me, let him deny himself and take up his cross daily and follow me" (Luke 9:23). Jesus also predicted that his followers would face suffering and persecution just like he did, but he promised to be with us and to send us the Holy Spirit to strengthen us (see, for example, Matt 10:16–39). Trusting in this promise, we try to accept our sufferings patiently and pray that God will give us the grace to persevere in them. This requires fortitude (or courage). Fortitude is a moral virtue that we can develop that allows us to stand firm against temptation, trial, and suffering. It is perfected by a gift of the Holy Spirit that we receive in Baptism and Confirmation.

The example of Jesus the Suffering Servant also shows us that our suffering can be a source of redemption. As we saw above, Jesus' suffering was not in vain. Offered as a sacrifice, it became the source of our salvation. In the same way, our suffering is never meaningless, because we are able to participate in his sacrifice by uniting our suffering to his. This is why St. Paul says, "Now I rejoice in my sufferings for your sake, and in my flesh I complete what is lacking in Christ's afflictions for the sake of his body, that is, the Church" (Col 1:24). St. Paul isn't saying that Jesus' sufferings on the Cross are insufficient for our salvation. Rather, he is emphasizing his responsibility to unite his sufferings to Christ on behalf of the Church. We have that same privilege. Our sufferings, united to Jesus' suffering on the Cross, are a form of penance, which can help make up for the temporal consequences of sins. We can offer our trials and tribulations to God for our own benefit in moving us closer to the kingdom or on behalf of others for the graces they may need in their earthly struggle.

Jesus on the Cross is our example, but we know that the Cross was not the end of Jesus' story. He rose! He walked out of the tomb on the third day, alive! He ascended into heaven, bringing human flesh into communion with the immaterial God. He sits victorious, as we say in the Nicene Creed, "at the right hand of the Father." If we participate in the redemptive action of Christ, as St. Paul describes above, we, too, will share in the victory of Christ: heaven, eternal life, and a new creation.

Isn't Making Sacrifices and Putting up with Suffering a Sign of Weakness?

No. Making sacrifices and enduring suffering requires true courage and strength. Again, Jesus is our example. Even though, as the Son of God, he is all-powerful, Jesus came among us a servant (Luke 22:27; Phil 2:7), giving us an example of selfless love. This freedom from selfishness and sin didn't come from weakness but from strength. It allowed Jesus to face down the temptations of the devil and the power of the Jewish and Roman authorities, all while remaining faithful to his mission. Through this fidelity and by accepting the Father's will even in the face of the terrible suffering of the Cross, Jesus won the victory over sin and death and rose from the dead.

We are called to follow his example, and he gives us the grace to do so. As we grow in holiness and virtue, we leave sin behind and become less concerned with our own comfort. This, too, isn't a weakness but a strength. Jesus tells us that "every one who commits sin is a slave to sin" (John 8:34). While it might feel like freedom to just do whatever we want or whatever feels good, sin and selfishness are like addictions that enslave us. As we become more and more concerned with preserving our pleasures or our comfort or our ego, our will grows weak and we find it harder and harder to avoid sin. Virtue and holiness, on the other hand, free us to do what is right, even when it means sacrificing pleasure or comfort.

Trusting in God's will as Jesus did in the Garden of Gethsemane gives us courage. We know that, whether we see it in this life or the next, the final victory belongs to God, and this frees us from obsession with our own self-preservation to follow Jesus, even in great difficulty. This even gives us the power to follow Jesus' command to "Love your enemies and pray for those who persecute you" (Matt 5:44). As St. Paul tells us, our trust in God's justice frees us from the need to seek revenge so that we are not overcome by evil, but can overcome evil with good (Rom 12:19–21).

In this way, facing suffering is a necessary part of growing in faith. It tests us and pushes us to free ourselves from attachment to our will and comfort. This gives us the power not only to endure suffering but even to rejoice in it, knowing that God can use it for our own good and his glory.

In the End, Isn't It Really Only the Final Result That Matters?

Every moral choice we make is significant. As Pope St. John Paul II explains:

> Human acts are moral acts because they express and determine the goodness or evil of the individual who performs them. They do not produce a change merely in the state of affairs outside of man but, to the extent that they are deliberate choices, they give moral definition to the very person who performs them, determining his *profound spiritual traits.* This was perceptively noted by Saint Gregory of Nyssa: "All things subject to change and to becoming never remain constant, but continually pass from one state to another, for better or worse. . . . Now, human life is always subject to change; it needs to be born ever anew. . . . But here birth does not come about by a foreign intervention, as is the case with bodily beings . . . ; it is the result of a free choice. Thus *we are* in a certain way our own parents, creating ourselves as we will, by our decisions."[1]

In other words, our moral decisions shape us so that through our own free choices, we form our moral life, just as our parents formed our physical life. This is because whenever we make a choice we aren't just choosing to *do* a particular thing; we also are choosing to *be* a particular kind of person. So, when you choose to steal or gossip or look at por-

[1] Pope John Paul II, Encyclical Letter Regarding Certain Fundamental Questions of the Church's Moral Teaching *Veritatis Splendor* (August 6, 1993), §71.

nography, you are, at least to some extent, choosing to be the kind of person who does those things. Likewise, when you choose to give generously or speak charitably or live chastely, you are choosing to be a person who is generous, charitable, and chaste. Over time, when we repeat these choices, they become good or bad habits—virtues or vices—that become ingrained in our character.

Every moral choice has some effect on us, and it has an effect on others as well. The effect that our choices have on others is obvious in some cases: when we steal or gossip we harm someone else's goods or reputation; when we are generous and loving in our speech, we make life better for others. Even things that seem like minor sins—for instance, lying or cheating in small ways—have an effect on others. Human society is built on trust and cooperation, so even small acts of dishonesty or selfishness undermine that trust.

Even when our choices don't have an obvious direct effect on others, though, they have an indirect effect through the way they shape our character. For instance, if we choose to harbor jealous, hateful, or lustful thoughts, these may not directly harm another person, but they shape our character in a way that makes it harder for us to resist temptations to sins that do directly affect others. If, on the other hand, we continually direct our mind toward thoughts that are generous and loving, this helps form virtuous habits, which make it easier for us to be generous and loving toward others. In this way, every choice we make is morally significant because it shapes our own character and our relationships with others.

Thus, what makes a choice morally good is not the final result (which we often can't predict or fully control). Nor is it enough to just have good intentions. For a choice to be morally good, both our intentions and the thing we are choosing must be good. In other words, a good end does not justify an evil means. We may not do evil that good may come of it. Even if the end result does turn out all right, we have still chosen to do evil, and this choice morally shapes us.

The temptation to do evil for the sake of achieving a good result can sometimes be strong. Overcoming this temptation requires growing in virtue and praying for the graces discussed in the previous two questions.

So, we have to be willing to face suffering ourselves rather than choose to do what is wrong. We also need to be ready to face pressure and criticism from others, because many people *do* believe that the end justifies the means and they won't understand our moral stand. Finally, we need humility and trust in God. This lets us realize that we can never fully predict or control the future, so we must always do what is right, trusting that God has the power to protect us and bring good even out of the worst situations.

Conclusion

Throughout this course we have studied the Paschal Mystery of the Passion, death, and Resurrection of Jesus Christ and the effects of this mystery upon ourselves and the world. Jesus teaches us about God's deep love for us and his desire for our salvation. He also teaches us about ourselves. Through our encounter with Jesus in the Gospels, we come to learn about who we are called to be. He models for us what it means to be a fully mature, fully alive human being and leaves us with the challenge to "be perfect, as your heavenly Father is perfect" (Matt 5:48). Through God's grace, we are able to answer that challenge, growing in Christian maturity even amid periods of trial and suffering, with hope-filled joy and anticipation of the coming of God's kingdom.